D1131269

Great houses

Great houses

for view sites
beach sites
sites in the woods
meadow sites
small sites
sloping sites
steep sites
and flat sites

(AR) AN ARCHITECTURAL RECORD BOOK

EDITED BY WALTER F. WAGNER JR., AIA

EDITOR, ARCHITECTURAL RECORD

McGraw-Hill Book Company

New York   St. Louis   San Francisco   Auckland   Düsseldorf   Johannesburg   Kuala Lumpur   London   Mexico
Montreal   New Delhi   Panama   Paris   São Paulo   Singapore   Sydney   Tokyo   Toronto

The editors for this book were
Jeremy Robinson and Hugh S. Donlan,
and the designer was Jan V. White

It was set in Optima by Quinn & Boden Company, Inc., Rahway, N.J.
It was printed by Halliday Lithographic Corporation
and bound by The Book Press

Library of Congress Cataloging in Publication Data
Main entry under title:

Great houses for view sites, beach sites, sites in the
   woods, meadow sites, small sites, sloping sites, steep
   sites and flat sites.

   "An Architectural record book."
   Includes index.
   1. Dwellings—United States. 2. Architecture,
Domestic—Designs and plans. 3. Architecture, Modern—
20th century—United States. I. Wagner, Walter F.
II. Architectural record.
NA7208.G73   728.3   75-12859
ISBN 0-07-002314-X

34567890HDBP78543210987

Contents

4: HOUSES FOR SITES IN THE WOODS — 94

5: HOUSES FOR SMALL LOTS — 128

Great houses for great sites

*If only we could have a house with a beautiful view . . . If only we could have a
house with a brook rolling by . . . or in the mountains . . .
or up on the hillside looking down over the city.
If only we could have a house like . . . If only . . .*

You can, of course. If you care enough about it. As I wrote in an earlier book in this series: "A house is (or can be, or should be) perhaps the most personal expression of your life. . . . There is something very special about a house that is special for you—which is why some people look so hard for houses and don't buy the first fake Colonial that comes along in a town with a good school and a neighborhood with a reputation for good resale value; and why some people go and find a good architect and enter on the time-consuming, mind-bending, sometimes frustrating, but always rewarding process of having their own house designed and built just for them.

"Living in an everyday kind of house—compared with a house that really fits your way of living, on the kind of site that you like best—must be like being married to a woman who has never learned to cook well; you can get used to it, but you miss something every day of your life."

If the most important things to you are status and ready resale value, you know where to find them. But . . .

**If you want a house
just right for your family,
you begin by finding
the site that is just right**

If you have the courage and the fortitude and strong sense of personal identity that it takes to be thinking about a custom-designed house (as most readers of this book will be), it is fair to say that you *can* have that house that is just right . . . and that is on just the right kind of site. You can have a house that makes such sensitive use of that site that not just your eye is rewarded, but your whole sense of well-being, your sense of enjoyment of life.

an introduction

Making the most of the site, whatever that site is, is the starting place for the design of most really good houses. Most of the houses in this book have some kind of view and, because they were designed by skillful architects, make sensitive use of that view. And that sense of "being just right for this piece of land" is perhaps the most important difference between architect-designed houses and built-for-sale houses.

Of course you can't have just the kind of land you want. Or can you? It all depends on how strong your urge is to have the kind of land you like best.

There is, to be obvious about it, no way that even a highly skillful architect in most parts of the country can give you a view of the sea rolling in. But there are, of course, millions of people for whom living by the ocean is so important that they insist on living in that narrow band of land in our coastal states and would not move without an extraordinary incentive.

Similarly, there are millions of people who feel so strongly about "their kind of country"—be it mountains (lots of those), or desert, or lake, or tumbling stream, or the vitality of a city twinkling below—that they choose to live there and make considerable sacrifices to do so. Many (indeed an increasing number of young people) refuse the regular transfers around the country intended to make them the compleat corporate executive. Many commute long distances by train or car from city jobs to get to "their kind of place." And many people (maybe they're the lucky ones) refuse the lure of jobs in the city and choose to live on their kind of land at great financial sacrifice.

So if you really want to live on a mountain, go find one to live on—and if there aren't any in your part of the country, at least find yourself a hillside. They are available everywhere. In 90 per cent of this country, you can find a stream or lake or meadow to live on. You may have to make some trade-offs in terms of time or convenience . . . but you can find "your kind of land."

Isn't special land
much more expensive?
Sure it is.
But . . .

That lovely site—on a stream, or with a great view—may be twice or three times as expensive as featureless sites nearby. Suppose, to pick a nice, round, staggering number, the land is $10,000 more expensive. Too much? Look at it this way:

That's about $100 a month on the mortgage. You can save some of that on the house. Or give up your vacation. If you like your house and land well enough, why go away? (People who live on Cape Cod, or in Aspen, have something going for them.) Drive the old car for three more years, and you've a minimum of $5,000 towards the cost of that "expensive land." It's all in your priorities. Think about it.

This is not to say that your "land with a view" *has* to be more expensive. One notable exception (and you'll find many examples in this book): steep land. Steep sites—not just in rural areas but sometimes even close to downtown—are often by-passed as "too difficult" or even "impossible to build on." Some of the most exciting houses in this book were built on that "impossible" land. What's impossible to a builder who must keep on schedule, or who can't get involved in special foundations, is not impossible to an imaginative architect and client. Sure, the foundation work will be expensive—but maybe the lower cost of the land will offset that. It happens all the time.

**Once you've found
just the right land,
then make the house
just right for the land**

Royal Barry Wills, the architect who did so many wonderful houses in New England, once told me that the ideal way to site a house would be to camp out on the land for several weeks in each of the four seasons—to see what it was like on a hot summer day, on a rainy day, on a fall day, on a windy day, on a day with three feet of snow on the ground.

While this is of course not practical, Mr. Wills did, as a matter of principle, begin the design of many houses he designed by spending several days visiting the site—"mostly just smoking my pipe," but also making notes and sketches. He used a broad felt pen "so I couldn't get too fussy in my thinking." In a letter he wrote me

20 years ago, he said, "If you're going to live in a house for 20 or 30 or 50 years, it's worth a good many days of thinking before you even start to fool with designs. There's one right place for the house, and what you've got to do is find it."

And only when you and your architect have found the right land and the right place on that land for the house, does house design begin.

**While there are few
hard-and-fast rules,
a certain kind of house
makes sense for
every different kind of site**

In the chapters that follow, we'll discuss in detail some of the forms, and materials, and massing ideas, that make a house right for various sites—right for a beach site, or a site in the woods, or a meadow, or a gently or steeply sloping site. To be obvious about it, a good mountain cabin would not only look foolish on a beach, it wouldn't work. The design of most good houses *begins* with the site; and thus the house grows out of the site, is appropriate for that site—in short, looks as if it belonged there.

And while there are—as you'll see in the chapter introductions that follow—some general rules for making a house "the right kind of house" for each of the different kinds of sites, you'll find that for any kind of site you have plenty of options left.

The houses shown in each chapter—all designed by architects—are all very different in detail, in orientation, in plan, in degree of openness, and in materials used. The reason is simple: as a house that is just right for one family can seldom be just right for another, a house that is just right for one site cannot, almost by definition, be right for another.

—Walter F. Wagner Jr.

1: Houses for sites with a

Houses on any of the varied sites described in this book are likely to have a view. A house with a view! Surely this is one of the most universal of the dreams of prospective homeowners. But making the best use of that view is not a simple design matter. It involves the kind of view—and the kind of person you are. For example, you can make *too much* of the view. There's a big temptation to want "lots of glass opening the whole house to the view." But think about it. You've probably had dinner in one of those restaurants on top of a tall building, maybe even one of the currently in-vogue revolving ones. They're sort of fun to visit, but would you really like to live there? The sea is magnificent to watch—but most sailors would tell you that the view of the sea is so vast and so overpowering that you really don't want to live with it all the time. I've often thought that it would take a pretty special kind of powerful personality to be comfortable living on top of a mountain, gazing down at the world below. Or take the opposite extreme: living in a quiet, shaded glen by a rushing stream. Lots of people would hate living in a perennially shaded place—trees are beautiful, but too many trees mean little sunlight, few flowers, no grass. And not a half-mile from my house in Connecticut is a lovely little house built close to a perfectly beautiful waterfall—which gets a new owner about every two years. The reason: the noise! The sound of a waterfall can be a joy on a picnic afternoon, but the sound of a waterfall every evening, every night when you're trying to go to sleep, every morning the second you wake up, and then while you're having breakfast, and then when you go out to get the mail. . . . You get the point.

Wind is another factor. Many sites with great views are by their nature exposed to the wind—on the seashore, in certain gullies, atop high hills. Most sailors, again, would tell you that there are times when you feel sure you'll go out of your mind if the sound of the wind doesn't stop now! On Cape Cod, for instance, most weekend visitors describe the wonderful cool sea breeze; most residents know that on many summer afternoons the breeze reaches 20 miles per hour, and after the first three days it really gets on their nerves.

If you'll study the houses on the next pages (and again, throughout the book, since most of the houses have a "view" in the broad sense I've described above), you'll find that few of them "give it all" to the view. Most do, indeed, open to the view—most often in the main living spaces. But, often, the quieter rooms—the dining room and the bedrooms—either face away from the view or open to a "quieter" view: a view along the hillside, or back into the hillside, or to the meadow leading down into the lake instead of the lake itself. Often, such rooms open to a sheltered terrace or patio. Special attention is often given to dining areas—somehow, a spectacular view down a chasm isn't right for while you're eating.

Most people require a sense of shelter part of the time—no matter how much they love their "big view."

Outdoor living is a related problem that has to be thought about carefully. The reason that "California living" started in California is that California is one of the few places where the climate is right for true indoor-outdoor living any appreciable part of the year.

Some people love outdoor living—and they should make decks and terraces and patios an important part of their design for a new house. But if you don't really like outdoor living—think about it!—then don't spend a lot of money for outdoor living spaces. Personally, I love the outdoors—hiking, skiing, and especially sailing. But I don't like to eat out-of-doors. Un-American as it seems to some of my friends, I hate to cook steaks on a charcoal grill and would much prefer to have the meat cut up and prepared with onions and red wine and celery and mushrooms and carrots and herbs and then eat it sitting at the dining room table.

The way you really want to live—not the way you think you should live or what the magazines tell you is "the life style"—is an important consideration in the design of your house.

And the placement of that outdoor living space is critically important. In many thoughtlessly designed houses, a wooden deck is positioned just outside sliding glass doors from the living room. That's fine in many instances, but . . .

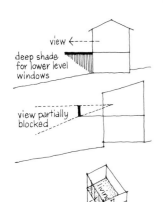

In a two-story house, a second-level deck makes a dungeon out of the rooms below. On many hillside or other view sites, the deck and its railing spoil the view. Opening the deck to the side is often the best solution—giving both the indoor space and the outdoor space the same view.

Orientation is another key consideration in taking advantage of a view. I suppose (never thought about it before) that something like one-quarter of the views from houses are north, one-quarter east, and so on. Though (come to think of it) the vast majority of houses with views over the Pacific Ocean must face west, and houses with Atlantic views face either south or east. Those orientations spell, to any architect, very different problems. What you get with a stunning view of the Pacific Ocean is a real sun problem all afternoon. The morning sun that greets early risers along the Atlantic Coast is typically welcome, and requires much less design attention. The ski house on the north side of a mountain has to be different from a house just a short schuss away on the southern slope—and, unless they are different, one owner or another must be getting less than he could have. Making the most of a site while handling the problems of orientation or siting is one of the things that good architects do for their clients.

The nine very different houses in this first chapter show nine very different view sites: you'll find a woodland house that explores views of the forest in all directions; a house in an urban neighborhood that has a spectacular view of the city below; a house on a spectacular site in Europe, where they have known how to take advantage of mountain views for a thousand years (and built with little regard for cost, thus offering some extraordinary ideas about living on a great site); a lovely little house in a meadow by an Irish lake; and four houses for mountain-country sites that, while they began with similar problems and opportunities, are entirely different in their development and design.

A HOUSE WITH A VIEW OVER THE CITY BELOW

Remo Pratini photos except as noted

Edmund Burger

Patricia Coplans' hillside house in San Francisco rises in a conspiracy of angled planes and projections to overlook Golden Gate Park and the Pacific Ocean. The projecting bay windows are part of a local residential tradition but the sloping window walls (photos right) are a direct response to particular site conditions and the architect-owner's desire to capture as much sunlight as possible on this steeply contoured north slope.

The plan is compact and simply ordered in spite of the visual complications created by the projections. The living room occupies the north end of the house over the garage and is overlooked, in turn, by a gallery level guest bedroom. Master bedroom and bath occupy the second floor over the kitchen. The sloping glass roof of the dining area frames a view up the slope of tall stands of eucalyptus. A central entry hall, also skylighted, is reached from the garage below or by a winding outdoor stair on the west side of the house.

Finish materials are sympathetically selected and detailed with skill. Exterior walls are Western Cedar nailed up in diagonals that echo the slope of the site in two directions. Interior partitions are gypsum board over wood studs; flooring is teak parquet for the living room and clay tile for dining room and kitchen. Rich accents, like the marble fireplace surround, are used sparingly. A dark red baked enamel finish, used on all gutters, downspouts, window sash corner details and roof, contrasts warmly with the cedar siding, and gives the house a crisp, firm-edged angularity. This linear emphasis is restated inside in the window and door trim as in the unusually crisp and elegant skylight details.

The Coplans house is invested with a stimulating spatial character—a character that is personal but not aberrant, a character that does not dissolve with the second or third look.

Architect and owner: Patricia A. Coplans of Burger and Coplans. *Location:* San Francisco, California. *Engineers:* Geoffrey Barrett (structural); James Peterson (mechanical). *General contractor:* Patricia Coplans.

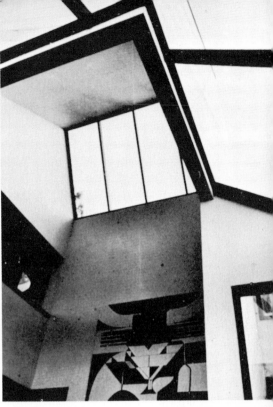

The furnishings in the Coplans' house are a mixture of built-ins and modern classics in chrome, cane and leather. The relative formality of many of these pieces is surprising but no problems of compatability seem to arise.

Large skylights in many spaces flood the house with light but glazing is tinted for protection against the sun's direct rays.

Outdoor, cantilevered viewing decks, a dining room balcony and a bedroom loft help make this cedar-clad house for a family of three an always delightful and practical place to live.

The carefully organized house is a successful outcome of architect Hobart Bett's design thinking, which he expresses with the same verve that is evident in the design itself. "It's a spatial ballgame," he explains, "within a very disciplined order." The idea was to create "pretty straightforward relationships, very tight, very well organized in plan, which make, in section, spatial complication—with spaces going in, out, up, down, and ducking around. All this is done within a very specific architectural framework that is recognizable, that pulls all the spaces back." Thus, fireplace and stairs are grouped to permit a tight-knit organization of space, and to provide a tall, visual anchor for the house. Rooms double back, and open onto each other, but are all disposed off, and relate back to, the scissor stair. A resulting "balance between serenity and excitement" is paired with a balance between economy and

Master bedroom loft (above) overlooks living room (below). Dining balcony can be seen to rear of photo. Livingroom opens onto deck oriented to the south and for a close-range view of trees; fourth-level dining deck, much higher by virtue of the sharp incline, is oriented for morning sun and a long-range view of mountains to the east. Entry at mid-level takes best advantage of the slope. Exterior random width cedar siding carries throughout interior. The roof is cedar shingles; the basic structure, platform wood frame. Vertical organization of spaces and the use of cantilevers helped keep the cost of the foundation and site work down.

Norman McGrath photos

space: The idea is "to take things that are in fact small and artfully relate them suddenly to give them magnitude," the architect explains. Thus, the dining room is just 9 feet by 12, but, as the section and plan above suggest, borrows space from the living room it overlooks, to give

the impression of being twice that size. All is done, finally, "to exploit the unique qualities of the land," and, of course, to meet the owners' needs. Thus the site, a sharply sloping hill, suggested the orientation, and the basic vertical economical organization of the design. Projecting

decks exploit views of mountains and close-up views of trees. And by isolating children's bedroom, guest and playroom on the lowest levels (see section) the architect was able to "play" with the upper three levels for the parents use, while zoning as required.

Architect: Hobart D. Betts—Moulton Andrus, project architect. *Owners:* Mr. and Mrs. George C. McCune, Jr. *Location:* Londonderry, Vermont. *Structural engineer:* Stanley Gleit. *Mechanical engineer:* Peter Flack. *Contractors:* George C. McCune, Jr. and P. William Polk, Jr.

A POWERFUL HOUSE FOR AN OVERPOWERING VIEW

This extensive residence for one of Europe's foremost publishers is isolated almost 2,000 feet above Lago Maggiore in southern Switzerland. The magnificent lake view, however, becomes visible only after one has passed through the entrance hall and into the living rooms which have spacious balconies facing toward the south and east and the lake below. As in many of his designs, the architect protects the rim of such high, elevated balconies and terraces by wide and shallow "waterguards." As reflecting pools these "waterguards" mirror the clouds during the day and at night the moonlit mountain silhouette.

All rooms of the house are skillfully oriented to some aspect of mountain landscape. At the same time, the architect has insured a feeling of intimacy in a variety of places within each room. With intimacy in mind, he has most ingeniously created a kind of cavernous, quiet pool below the house which can be utilized in all seasons.

Architect: Richard J. Neutra; job captain: Egon Winkens; resident architect: Bruno Honegger. Location: Sopra Navegna, Switzerland.

The inner and outer portions of the pool are separable by pushing a button and turning up a "submarine" trap door. The pool is heated according to comfort. Above the living quarters of the first two floors, there is a top story and a terrace. The surrounding roofs are flooded with water, insulating the house in summer and mirroring the changes of color in the sky and the mountain landscape. To Neutra, this effect offers a visual and psychological linkage to the waters of Lago Maggiore far below: further proof of the architect's remarkable skill in relating a house to its landscape.

photo below by Alberto Flammer; all others by Hesse

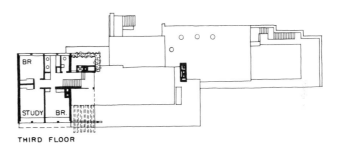

BR   STUDY   BR

THIRD FLOOR

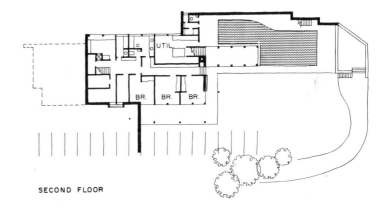

UTIL   BR.   BR.   BR.

SECOND FLOOR

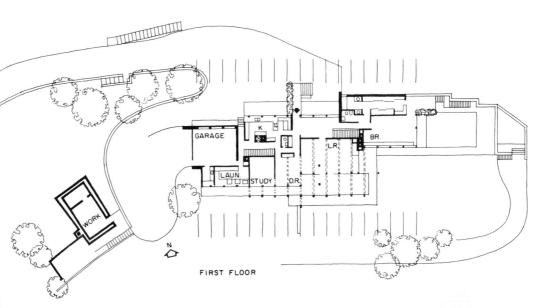

GARAGE   K   LAUN   STUDY   D.R.   L.R.   BR.

WORK

N

FIRST FLOOR

The fireplace is composed of a raised hearth slab and a stainless steel hood. Living quarters open onto a waterguarded balcony terrace where the usual protective railings have disappeared and one's view is unimpeded. The same detail exists at the windows of the private suite of master bedroom, dressing room and bath.

Norman R. C. McGrath photos

A HOUSE FOR A QUIET RIVERSIDE

Perched on reinforced concrete stilts on a hillside overlooking the river Brandon in southwest Ireland, with a distant view of the Irish Sea, this little concrete and glass weekend house combines strength and elegance to a remarkable degree for so small a structure. Although the house is only a 36-foot square, extensive use of glass on all sides and open planning give an unusually spacious effect. The fireplace and storage wall separates the bedroom from the living area—providing privacy without total enclosure. Even though the house is used only for weekends and vacations, it contains a collection of classic modern furniture which admirably complements the uncluttered interiors.

Architect: Robin Walker of Michael Scott & Partners. *Owner:* Mr. Michael P. O'Flaherty. *Location:* County Cork, Ireland. *Interior designer:* Patrick Scott.

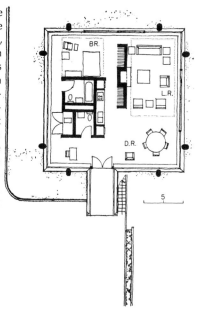

. . AND A SIMPLE HOUSE FOR A SKI HILL

Located on a hillside in the snow country of Vermont, this large vacation house was designed to accommodate with equal ease both large-scale parties and quiet family living —and to function as well as a summer retreat as for ski weekends. The solution could have been a rambling, over-whelming affair; instead, the seemingly conflicting require-ments have been unified under an elegantly simple and beautifully crafted shed roof form. The house seems rela-tively small, until one enters to see the great spaciousness which makes it work—and which compounds the pleasure of the hillside site.

Architect: Eliot Noyes & Associates. *Location:* Stratton, Vermont. *Mechanical engineers:* Dimartino Associates. *Interiors:* Eliot Noyes & Associates. *Contractor:* R. T. Arnold Lumber Company.

FRONT ELEVATION   5

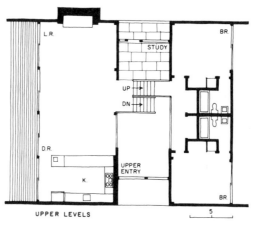

Hans Namuth photos

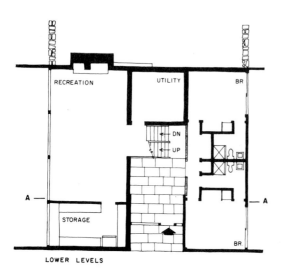

LOWER LEVELS

UPPER LEVELS

5

The architect's solution for the large house divides space while interlocking it, and the structure is rugged and secure against the elements but lets summer breezes penetrate throughout. Four levels are staggered off a central stair, and open into each other at the two-story entry hall to provide efficient zoning—and a dramatic spatial interest.

The skillfully executed scheme unifies interiors and structure in the over-all, plastic flow of space: warm textures and colors enhance the natural wood structural members; sleek built-ins and relaxed furniture groupings define uncluttered space usage within the open living scheme. Deeply recessed floor-to-ceiling glass lets most areas share light from different sources, and visually extends rooms onto the slopes.

16

A third-level living-dining space includes the fireplace grouping at one end (photo above left) and the kitchen (photo above) in a clearly defined but open plan. Comfortable furnishings include black leather upholstery, a Moroccan rug and natural woods. Kitchen activities are only partially screened, in keeping with an all-pervading air of informality. The stair landing opening onto the second-level entry can be seen in the photo at left, with the fourth level visible beyond. Living areas open onto a full-width deck for southern exposure and a hillside view.

All levels of the house open into the entry hall, shown in the photo, left. Living areas are on levels to the left, with bedrooms to the right. A small study can be glimpsed behind the stairs. In the master bedroom, lower left, white curtains, a dark brown spread and orange and yellow pillows complement the natural wood and complete the uncluttered scheme. The glass wall incorporates sliding doors, and is neatly framed between the joists for a dramatic indoor-outdoor sense of space. The structure of the house is wood frame with rough-sawn cedar siding and built-up roof. Floors are yellow pine except for vinyl asbestos in the game room and the flagstone entry hall. Deep overhangs provide weather protection. Sliding glass doors are recessed 7 feet 8 inches on the south to give a deck on the third level for added summer living space.

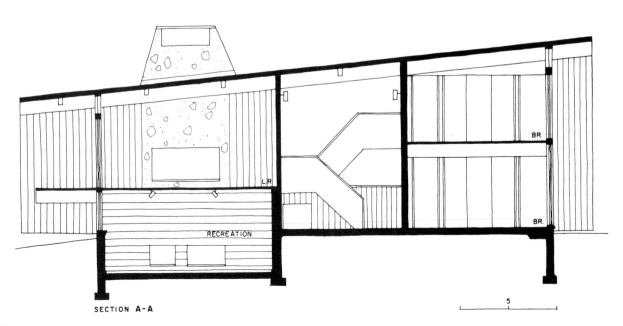

SECTION A-A

5

A MOUNTAINSIDE HOUSE OF MOUNTAINSIDE MATERIALS

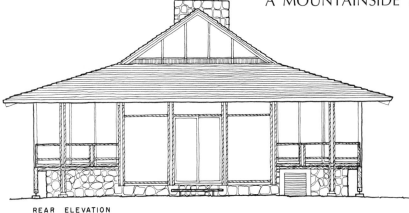

REAR ELEVATION

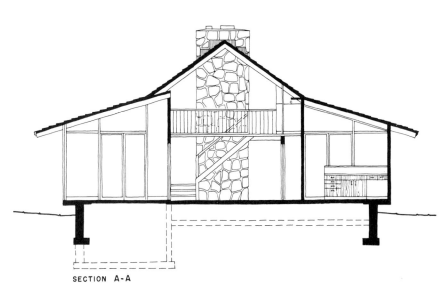

SECTION A-A

Wood, stone and the outdoors were the most powerful factors in determining the design of this house, which started with the tremendous advantage of a magnificent site on the front range of the Rockies near Boulder. Since the clients had deliberately moved out of the city to find seclusion in the mountains, they were naturally anxious to retain all the original features of the land, particularly the pine trees. Openings in several parts of the roof overhang allow the trees near the house to grow undisturbed, and are a very direct expression of the close relationship between house and site.

Architect Hobart Wagener rejected any temptation to compete with the surroundings and concentrated—most successfully—on designing a simple, logical structure "which would try to become an integral part of the site." For this purpose, cedar beveled siding and cedar shake roof were a good choice because of their attractive weathering quality. A bleaching oil finish was used on the walls to accelerate the natural process.

The sense of shelter and security needed in a fairly rugged setting is provided by placing the main seating area in a "well" between a raised terrace on one side and a raised dining area on the other, by the use of warm-colored brick for the floors, segmentation of the large glass areas, and the protective roof overhang all around the house.

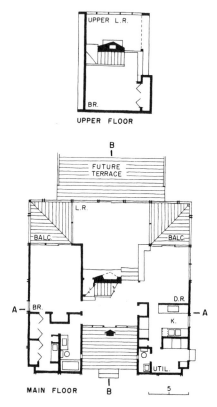

UPPER FLOOR

MAIN FLOOR

The interior is dominated by an enormous stone fireplace, an exposed ceiling structure and a dramatic view of the valley. Strategically placed clerestory windows highlight the effect of the ceiling formation and also point up the detailing of the fireplace stonework.

The house is small—with only one full bedroom on the first floor and a guest balcony behind the fireplace—but outdoor decks, the added height in the center of the house, and of course the view, extend the experience of space beyond its walls.

In addition to space and freedom, an exposed site of this kind demands warmth, shelter and a sense of permanence. This was fully recognized by the architect in the careful balance of openness and enclosure and in his sensitive exploitation of the strong, textural quality of natural materials.

Architects: Hobart D. Wagener Associates—*associate on job:* Robert E. Carlson. *Owners:* Mr. and Mrs. A. J. Bartkus. *Location:* Boulder, Colorado. *Contractor:* Warren R. Slattendale.

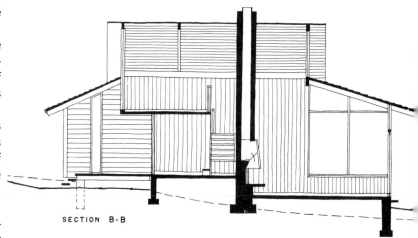

SECTION B-B

Phokion Karas photos.

LIVING

BR

KIT

DINING

BR

UPPER FLOOR   5

GAME   UTIL.   BR.

STUDIO   LAUN.   BR.

LOWER FLOOR

SIMPLE SQUARE BOX ON A MOUNTAINSIDE

This vacation house is good evidence of the continuing use of inventive and playful forms in the design of weekend retreats. Low cost and compact, it uses maintenance-free natural materials. Located on a rugged mountain site and oriented to take advantage of an impressive view to the west, this simple and compact weekend house was designed for both summer and winter use. All openings are deeply carved to form roof overhangs for protection from heavy snow. Steps to elevated decks provide easy access at any snow depth in winter. During the summer, the doors and windows open to the decks and the breeze. Deeply setback porch with cantilevered deck provides additional summer living space, cross ventilation and an impressive view to the west. To create a structure compatible with its rugged site, the architect utilized straight-forward form with strong detailing—shed roof, reverse board and batten siding, and cantilevered decks with heavy railing seats. The house has a compact plan basically divided into a sleeping zone and a living zone, separated by the service core. Two other considerations affected the design: a tight budget ($16,000 in 1967 with unfinished basement and exclusive of furnishings); and minimum maintenance as reflected in the materials used—interior wood ceilings, exterior redwood siding, and use of stains for trim.

Architect and *owner:* Andrew Daland. *Location:* West Bethel, Maine. *Contractor:* Grover & Jordan, Inc.

The ski lodge is oriented to a southerly view and the large porch extends a multipurpose living area for summer use.

Louis Reens photos

. . . AND
A SPECIAL SHAPE FOR
A SPECIAL VIEW

The use of wood scissor trusses, 7-feet on center fabricated from standard 2-by-4 studs with nailed joints, gives this ski lodge its distinctive form. A two-story, multi-activity living area for the owners and their four young children is located on a large deck riding above native stone walls. Large glazed doors along the southerly wall permit a panoramic view and open onto a porch which becomes an extension of the living room. Also located on deck level are the master bedroom, bathroom and cooking area, above which is an open loft for dormitory-style sleeping quarters for the children. Exterior and interior walls are either of native stone, which was available on the site, or board and batten, with exterior roof of handsplit cedar shakes. "The spatial development, structural system and general material usage," says the architect Gerard Cugini, "are a conscious effort to reflect in scale and construction techniques the simplicity and directness of barn enclosures."

Architect and interior designer: Gerard R. Cugini. *Owner:* Mr. and Mrs. Douglas P. Webb. *Location:* Newbury, New Hampshire. *Structural engineer:* Arthur Choo Associates, Inc. *Contractor:* Vahan Sarkisian.

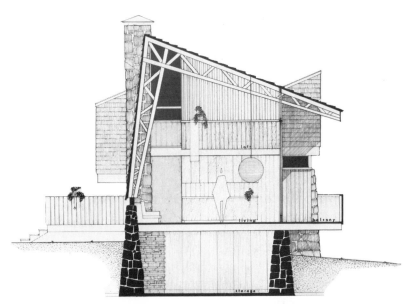

Wood scissor trusses define the two-level living room at one end of the building with sleeping areas, kitchen and bath stacked at the other end.

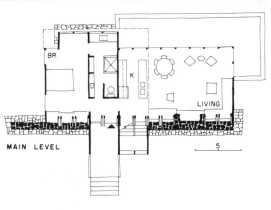

MAIN LEVEL   5

BR.   K.

LIVING

STOR.   CARPORT

UNEXCAVATED

LOWER LEVEL

2: Houses for beach sites

Sites on the beach are demanding in many ways, and have caused the development of a set of "rules" for beach-house design that are perhaps uniquely perfected. That is not to say that all beach houses are alike—far from it. Indeed, because of the vacation-house atmosphere associated with beach houses, there is a great deal of experimentation in new forms along our shorelines. But the conditions of sun and water and sand do a lot of dictating about the design.

Begin with the site. Because of the relative scarcity and desirability of waterfront land—especially on salt-water beaches—such sites tend to be very expensive and thus quite small. This develops an immediate problem of sound and visual privacy.

Again because of the scarcity of land, in many parts of the country there is a premium on land that is one, two, or more rows behind the best on-the-water land. And thus we see a tendency towards two-story houses that offer second-level living spaces and roof decks with a view—over the "blocking" front-row house—to the water. And even front-row houses are now tending to two stories on the smaller lots, in order to concentrate the living space on the lot and leave space for private outside gardens and decks.

In order to achieve desired privacy, many waterfront houses have essentially blank side walls and rear walls—while of course opening a maximum number of rooms to the view. Where zoning and building regulations permit it (and it is often permitted on beach sites), lots are often enclosed by high fences.

The design "rules" to which most beach houses are built include these:

1. Even on the beach, some kind of private courtyard or garden—shaded, private from passers-by on the beach, out of the wind and wind-blown sand—is increasingly common, and surely desirable. As suggested in the first chapter, the overpowering view of the ocean is sometimes "too much"—and the opportunity to be outdoors or in a more sheltered place is often welcome.

2. Screened porches or screened rooms are another welcome alternative to being out on the beach. In many parts of the country, at various times of the summer, insects are a maddening problem; and again even the minimal sense of shelter created by screening (and perhaps roll-down cloth wind screens) is frequently welcome.

3. On sandy sites, wooden decks are almost essential. Most people do not like to sit or lie for long on the sand—and the option of spreading out a mat on a deck raised above the sand is appealing. Further, on more than a few days of the summer, the sun heats the sand to a degree that few feet can stand. It is even desirable to be able to wet down decks—which means a hose bib.

4. Orientation to the breeze is critical. On most beach sites, the prevailing wind condition is quite constant, and, depending on the prevailing wind velocity, the house design must either invite the breeze in, or create shelter from it.

5. There must be some arrangement to cover and lock the windows, both for protection against heavy wind and to secure the house during the winter season. The early beach bungalows of course used shutters—but the larger glass areas of

contemporary beach houses (plus the larger incidence of break-ins, alas) suggest something more secure. One good device is solid wooden panels, hung from barn-door hardware, which slide across the openings and can, where necessary, be locked in place. In most parts of the country a beach house must be designed to withstand hurricane-force winds. Similarly . . .

6. It makes sense at most beach sites to assume that sooner or later water will be in the house. This suggests some high place, even in one-story houses, for storage of valuables, and an easy way to shut off all power to the house.

7. It is convenient to have a good storage area with doors opening to the outside for the storage of outdoor furniture, pads, and the mountain of paraphernalia—from life jackets to beach balls to umbrellas to kindling and drift wood—that gets collected at a beach house.

8. Exposed wall and roof framing is common in beach houses, and in many ways appropriate. But before you elect this "saving," be sure it is really what you want. If the house is not to look a bit "beach shack-y," the framing and wiring must be done with some degree of care.

9. Sand is a particular problem: you can't keep it out, so the sensible course is to make it easy to sweep it out—with a minimum of sills and perhaps trapdoors in the floor of each room. For this same reason, special attention must be paid to floors. Bare boards are fine, perhaps covered by those fiber rugs which are easily shaken out from time to time.

10. Materials are, of course, critical. Sidings of cedar, cypress, or redwood, or shingles of these materials, are the most common for obvious reasons. They withstand the moisture well and weather gracefully. Paint is, of course, a maintenance problem, but touches of paint—as in the trim and shutters of beach-front buildings—are traditional and welcoming.

11. Outside showers are a must in sandy areas. They should be screened so that the bather can undress completely. For the same reason, the outdoor shower should open either to a dressing room or a bathroom where clothes can be left.

12. Furniture? Wicker and canvas have been traditional for good reasons. They can be used by people in wet bathing suits, dry quickly, and are cool and comfortable.

13. In dune country, once construction is complete it's wise to plant grass to stabilize the sand. Rocks and stones from the beach can also be used to create appropriate rock gardens.

Well, any experienced user of beach houses could go on and on. About the need for a place for evening fires—perhaps a fireplace, but more often a Franklin stove or the newer free-standing units in contemporary shapes. About the need for closets and more closets. About valves positioned so you can turn off the water and drain the system for the winter. In the houses that follow, you'll find hundreds of other ideas to study and consider, as you consider your beach house. You'll find some "rule breakers"—including use of concrete on the beach that, in this house on this site, seems perfectly appropriate. And you'll find, as much for comparison purposes as anything else, two houses which are not strictly "beach houses." One is a house on a woodland lake, where the same kind of living is envisioned, but where the different site conditions (for example, no sand and no tide) drastically affect the siting and the appropriate use of materials. And there is a house for that most special of special sites, the rock-bound coast of Maine. As the description of this house says, "There is a strength and majesty to the granite sea wall of Maine that makes it impossible for any work of man to dominate—or indeed try to compete."

ON A CROWDED BEACH, A CENTRAL COURT FOR PRIVACY

A central court, with sub-spaces that pin-wheel around an existing sycamore, is the primary design feature in this Long Island residence by architect Hobart Betts. This outdoor space is decked in cedar, canopied by tree branches, and enclosed by the major elements of the house. Living, dining, kitchen and master bedroom functions are enclosed in the "L-shaped, shed-roofed structure on the north side and form a self-sufficient series of spaces when the owners are alone. Two guest bedrooms and a bath share the western side, and garage and storage complete the plan to the east (see plan).

Because the house is sited on a flat lot of modest size with no compelling views

and surrounded by neighboring houses, Betts settled on the court design and placed all major openings to the inside. This intro-version insures privacy for owners and guests while providing its users with an exceptionally pleasant outdoor space for entertaining on almost any scale.

Internal circulation is organized around the court and defined overhead by low, flat ceilings—a design device that heightens the sense of transition between inside and out and also offers a dramatic contrast to the high-ceilinged living, dining and sleeping spaces.

Betts has elected to relate this house to its two-story, neo-colonial neighbors by expressing the exterior walls as a continuous

plane wrapping around four sides and inter-rupted only where necessary to provide access to the central court. At these points (photo opposite top) the deck extends out-ward in the form of a tongue. The eleva-tions conceal the degree of fragmentation inherent in the plan but preserve an impor-tant sense of unity. Inside, this unity is achieved by a careful shaping of the spaces and a marvellously consistent use of materi-als, textures and finishes.

Architects: Hobart Betts Associates—Moulton Andrus, *project architect. Location:* Eastern Long Island. *Structural engineer:* Stanley Gleit. *Con-tractor:* Ralph L. Otis.

Maris-Semel photos

KIT.

GARAGE

L.R.

D.R.

STOR.

BR.

BR.

BR.

BR.

N ← 5

Construction is platform wood framing. Interior and exterior wall surfaces are rough-sawn cedar siding applied vertically throughout. Floors are white oak stained dark. Painted wood trim and cabinets contrast brightly with the rough-sawn cedar.

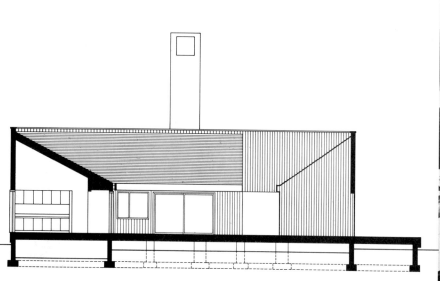

Maris-Semel photos

The corner condition, created by the intersection of tilted roof planes over the kitchen (photo right) has been handled with skill. The cabinet partition next to the dining table is kept away from the ceiling while the partition between kitchen and living room reaches full height to provide support for the dropped ceiling over the circulation space as it turns the corner.

A FLORIDA HOUSE ECHOES
THE SHAPE OF THE DUNES

Opposing triangular volumes butt against each other to create the strong massing in architect William Morgan's year-round house for his own family on Jacksonville, Florida's Atlantic Beach. Stepping down the flank of a primary dune, on an ecologically fragile site, the house opens at every level toward the ocean but maintains its privacy with blind walls at the sides and rear.

The entry level contains living and dining spaces, kitchen and garage. Parents' bedroom and work area are on the mezzanine above, and bunkrooms for the Morgans' two teenage sons are set on the level below. A central stair, linking all the levels, introduces a powerful diagonal around which the principal spaces of the house take shape.

The simple geometry of the forms is carefully matched to the profile of the dune and is reinforced by the bleached wood siding laid up in a pattern of opposing diagonals. A system of concrete grade beams and slabs, built over pilings, supports the wood frame. The skill with which the Morgan house is fitted to its site accounts for a good deal of its success. But just as important is the clarity with which the architect has developed his ideas and made them hold up, without noticeable compromise, through construction and final finishing.

When first published as a project, the house drew criticism from several correspondents who felt the site had been treated without sufficient regard for its ecological sensitivity. Some said the site should not have been built on at all. Such questions may still fairly be raised, but the continued stability of the dune, the return of the dune grasses and other plant and animal life are all encouraging.

Architect and owner: William Morgan. *Location:* Atlantic Beach, Florida. *Structural engineers:* Haley W. Keister Associates, Inc. *Lighting consultants:* William Lam Associates. *Contractor:* Ross Construction Company.

DR.
BR.   D STUDY

UPPER PART
OF L.R. & DR.

UPPER LEVEL   →N

KIT.
D

D.R.   L.R.

MAIN LEVEL

BR.   BR.

LOWER LEVEL   5

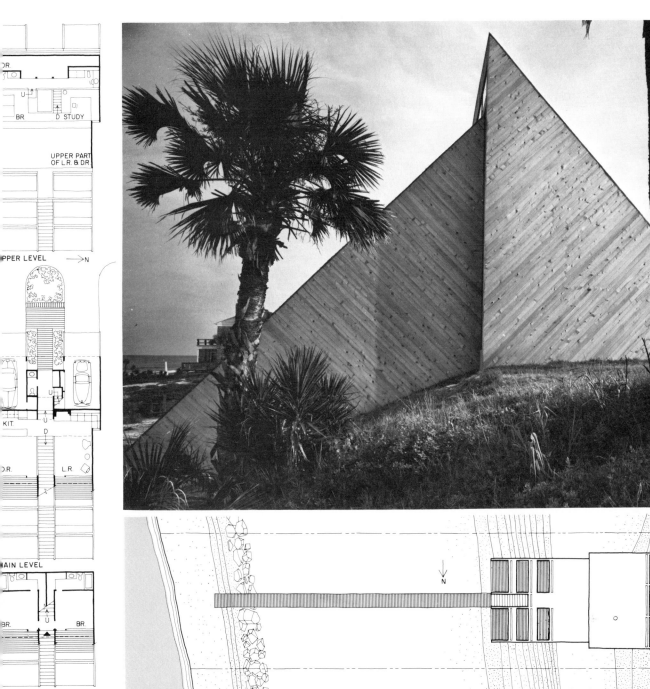

Daylight penetrates deep into the interiors. The main spaces are indirectly backlighted from high clerestory (see section perspective, at right). The outer sidewalls are washed with light from vertical strip windows at the juncture of the two triangular volumes. Together, these various sources generate a pleasant level of natural light throughout the house.

Tom Yee photos (courtesy of House & Garden)

Ronald Thomas photos

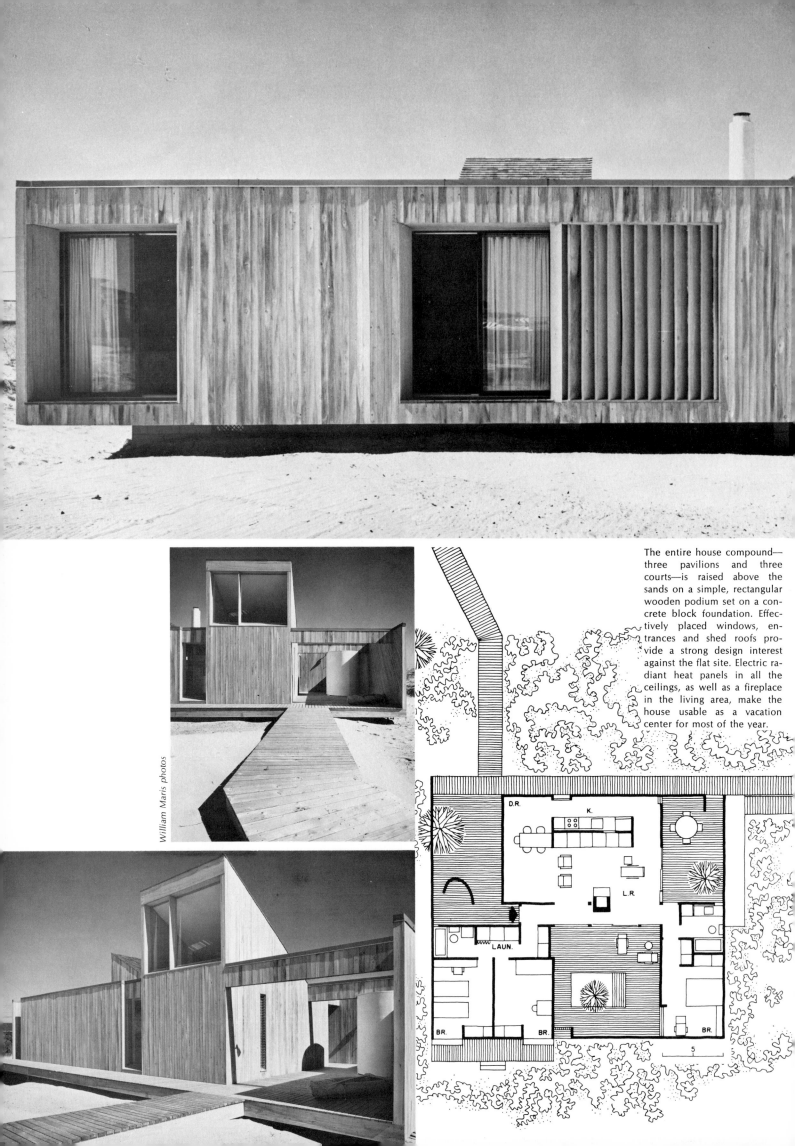

William Maris photos

The entire house compound—three pavilions and three courts—is raised above the sands on a simple, rectangular wooden podium set on a concrete block foundation. Effectively placed windows, entrances and shed roofs provide a strong design interest against the flat site. Electric radiant heat panels in all the ceilings, as well as a fireplace in the living area, make the house usable as a vacation center for most of the year.

D.R.   K.

L.R

LAUN.

BR.   BR.   BR.

5

PRIVACY AND APPROPRIATE MATERIALS FOR THE BEACH

As anyone visiting the more built-up beach resort areas to-day will undoubtedly be aware, closeness to the ocean is no guarantee of a good view—dunes and near-by houses often intervene. This crisp, sprightly-designed house creates its own completely private vistas by a three-zoned courtyard scheme. Linked pavilions for parents, children, and general living areas are adjoined by walled-in outdoor decks. High, shed-roofed clerestories are used to bring in more light and sun.

Simple, warm, easy to maintain materials were used throughout the house. Most walls, in and out, are natural cy-press treated with bleaching oil; the roof is partly built-up, partly shingled. Small-scaled quarry tiles form floors for all rooms but the bedrooms, which are carpeted.

Though definitely planned as an informal "second house," the design is a skilled combina-tion of comfortable practicality and sophistication. Bright col-ored fabrics, carpets and plants are used in all rooms to add a note of freshness to the neutral tones of the basic structure.

With all of the house's care-fully planned privacy, one is never conscious of being cut off from the outdoors when inside: sufficient windows are used to augment the big clerestories and the glass walls opening on the decks. Each area of the house has a direct outside en-trance for convenience in re-turning from the beach, and an outdoor shower is provided at the main entrance behind a curved screen-wall.

Much of the furniture in the house, including the long sofa, dining tables, cabinets and the like, are built-in to give an add-ed sense of order and space to the rooms. The few movable pieces, mainly chairs and small tables, were chosen for lightness of scale and design as well as for simple durability.

Architects: Julian and Barbara Neski. *Owners:* Mr. and Mrs. Edward Gor-man. *Location:* Amagansett, New York. *Contractor:* John Weiss.

The visual interest created in the Gorman house by closely linking indoor and outdoor spaces, and by the bold changes in ceiling levels, can be readily seen in these details of the main living spaces. Though all the areas are open to each other for good circulation when entertaining large groups of people, each room has its own distinction and individuality. Sliding glass walls permit the living room to be opened wide to the two adjoining outdoor decks.

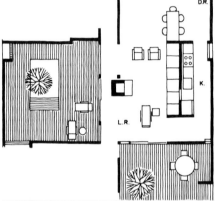

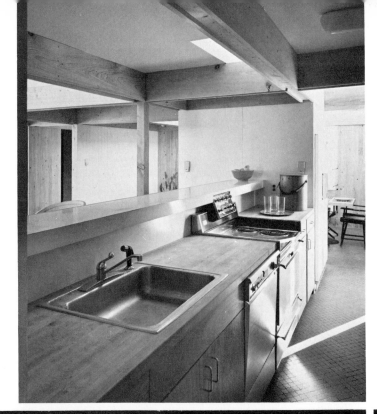

A SMALL BEACH HOUSE
OF STRIKING FORM

A low-lying site near an elevated drawbridge over the Shinnecock canal was chosen for this attractive cedar-shingle summer house. Private sleeping areas were required for a family of five, but the rest of the house is free-flowing, angular and exciting, with strategically placed windows and skylights giving good cross ventilation and unusual extension of visual space. Because of the possibility of flooding, the house is raised on piles, and a two-story solution was adopted to create a "positive visual relationship" with the dominant bridge structure. Decking around the house provides pleasant sunbathing areas and connects the main building with a detached storage house.

Architect: Hobart D. Betts. *Owners:* Mr. and Mrs. Hobart D. Betts. *Location:* Quogue, Long Island, New York. *Structural engineer:* Charles L. Sauer. *Interiors:* Glynne R. Betts.

Bill Maris photos (courtesy of Conde Nast)

SECOND FLOOR

FIRST FLOOR

Wade Swicord photos

A CONTEMPORARY VERSION OF THE TROPICAL HOUSE

Designed for a semi-tropical point of land at the mouth of an inlet to Sarasota Bay, this house represents an extremely convenient and contemporary version of the traditional columned, verandahed, broad-roofed house of the tropics. In this case, however, the columns are telephone poles, seven to a side, and the spaces above and below the raised living spaces are devoted to such modern amenities as a mechanical equipment core, storage rooms, bedroom and bath for maid or guests and sun decks and terraces. The three levels are contained within a simple square defined by a grid of full-height telephone pole structural members. The foundations consist of 18-foot creosote poles driven into the ground 12 feet apart, and capped with concrete at ground level. The floors are supported by heavy timber beams, and the roof is laminated, rough-sawn cedar decking covered with unpainted galvanized metal roofing. All of the walls, inside and out are either sliding glass panels or rough-sawn cedar siding. All structural members are left exposed, with considerable attention given

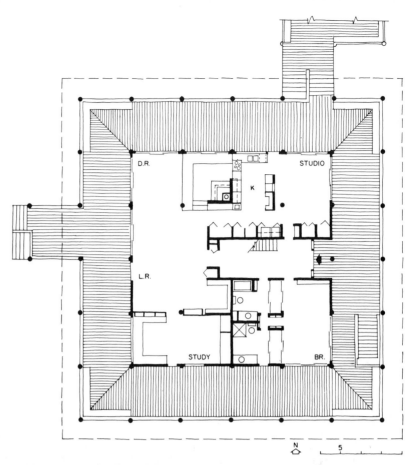

This atmospheric house was designed to provide permanent, year-round living and working quarters for the owners, and by the use of natural building materials and sympathetic forms, to quietly fit into its semi-tropical setting. All principal living spaces are on the main, raised level shown in the plan above. A free-standing staircase (photo left of plan) leads to an upper level containing storage space and a sun deck sunk into the roof. From the main-level verandah, a stair descends to a secondary square deck projecting from one corner of the house. The ground level contains a space for mechanical equipment, storage areas, and a small bedroom and bath; the remaining space at this level is gravel surfaced.

to the detailing of wall plane and pole junctures.

The natural condition of the site has been maintained, with the structure placed among existing palms, oak and mangrove. The raised living areas and verandahs surrounding the house afford a view of the Gulf from nearly every area in the house. Inside, all spaces except for bedrooms and baths, are defined by relatively low (8-foot-high) storage walls and by built-in furnishings, thus preserving most of the interior as a large, open space. The living spaces

formed in this manner include a generous living/dining area, a sunken conversation and fireplace pit, a kitchen area, a reading and lounging area, and two work studios. The entrance leads to a full height foyer which serves as a gallery for paintings and sculpture. The graveled space on the lower level serves for general outdoor living and as a carport.

Architect: Edward J. Seibert. *Associate architect:* D. Richmond. *Owners:* Mr. and Mrs. John D. MacDonald. *Location:* Sarasota, Florida. *Contractor:* Thyne Construction Company.

Wade Swicord photos

A LOW-LYING HOUSE ON THE BEACH

Architect Carl Abbott has designed an informal beach house on the Gulf of Mexico that also wraps around a lush tropical garden on the side away from the water. The main portion of the house, which is the winter residence of a New York couple who would rather be outside than in, is a raised platform for a better view of both the Gulf and the garden. It contains living rooms, the master bedroom and decks on every side. A second building, for frequent family visitors, is set in the garden itself and tied to the larger one by the stuccoed masonry walls that almost completely surround the complex.

Architect: Carl Abbott. *Owners:* Mr. and Mrs. David Weld. *Location:* an island near Sarasota, Florida. *Structural consultant:* A. L. Conyers. *Contractor:* W. C. Beall and Associates, Inc., Dale Pierce partner-in-charge.

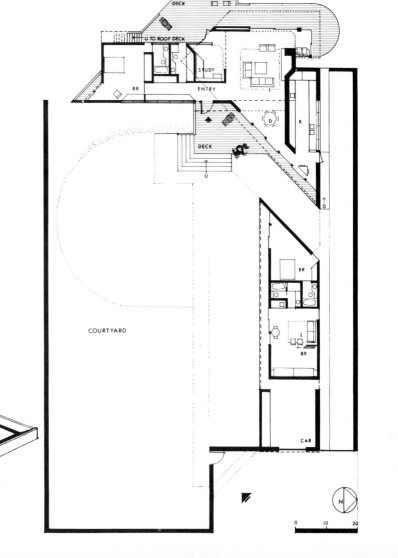

The living room and master bedroom (above) have views up and down the beach to the ends of the island as well as those of spectacular sun directly across the water. Horizontal rough cedar boards left to weather combined with the diagonal geometry give the house a rambling "beach shack" quality that is a surprising contrast to the more formal interior. During the day, light pours into the living room through the clerestory. At night (below), cove lighting echoes the natural effect.

A MULTI-LEVEL TOWER
ON THE BEACH

Great spaces and great views have made this beach house on Fire Island a luxurious yet fun place for a summer retreat. Only steps from the ocean, its two-story design of three interlocking octagons provide wide vistas of both bay and ocean. A soaring 24-foot living room is the focal point, with all other rooms tucked neatly around it, including two bedrooms with adjoining baths, kitchen, separate dining room, sauna bath and card playing "aerie." Decks and lookout roof terraces are spacious for sunbathing. For ease of upkeep, natural materials—Douglas fir and cedar siding—were used, painted surfaces were kept to a minimum, and most of the furniture built-in.

Architect: Earl Burns Combs. *Owner:* James Dines. *Location:* Fire Island Pines, New York. *Contractor:* Joseph Chasas.

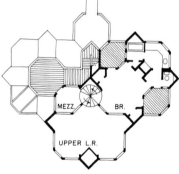

UPPER LEVEL

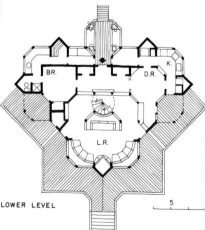

LOWER LEVEL

Bill Helms, photos

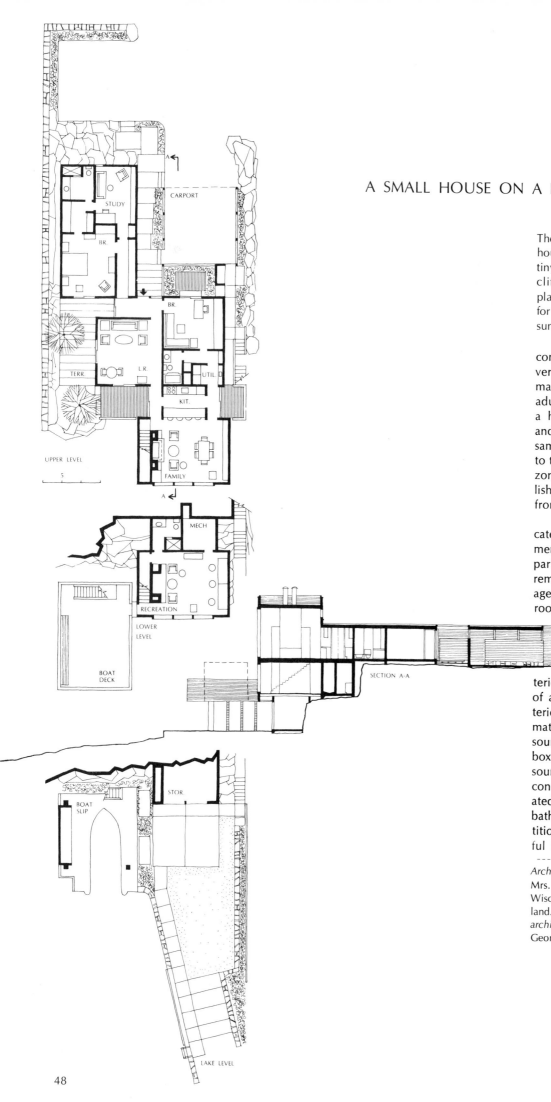

UPPER LEVEL

5

STUDY

BR.

CARPORT

BR.

TERR.

L.R.

UTIL.

KIT.

FAMILY

A

MECH

RECREATION

LOWER LEVEL

BOAT DECK

SECTION A-A

STOR.

BOAT SLIP

LAKE LEVEL

A SMALL HOUSE ON A DIFFICULT LAKEFRONT SITE

The many functions of an active lakeshore house are amply provided for here on a tiny lot which is split by a 25-foot rock cliff. This is a house of many different places—for eating, for visiting, for privacy, for swimming, for boating, for dancing, for sunning.

The architect, Edgar Wilson Smith, comments that "this lake community is a very active social area, with much informal, drop-in-type entertaining by both adults and teenagers. The owners wanted a house that would function naturally and easily in this situation, while at the same time affording a measure of privacy to those family members wishing it. Thus zoning and sound control was established as a major factor—against noises from within or without the house."

A glance at the plan quickly indicates how a somewhat unusual arrangement of the various rooms plays a large part in assuring that the parents' study remains quiet and peaceful during teen-age parties in the family room, recreation room or boat deck.

Noise transmission is also combatted by lining the house with sound-insulation board, which is used on both sides of all interior partitions, ceilings, and the inside of all exterior walls. In addition, all interior doors are equipped with "automatic door bottoms" to seal against sound; convenience outlets and switch box locations were chosen to minimize sound carry-through; heating and air-conditioning ducts are "sound attenuated"; and the daughter's bedroom and bath is isolated by a double-studded partition. The end results are very successful in assuring more quiet for all.

Architect: Edgar Wilson Smith. *Owners:* Mr. and Mrs. Art J. Priestley. *Location:* Lake Oswego, Wisconsin. *Structural engineer:* Bernard L. Tiland. *Contractor:* Barnard & Kinney. *Landscape architect:* Robert Hale Ellis, Jr. *Interior designer:* George M. Schwarz, Jr. and Associates.

Edmund Y. Lee photos

Norman McGrath photos

A HOUSE FOR A RUGGED ROCKY SHORELINE

There is a strength and majesty to the granite seawall of Maine that makes it impossible for any work of man to dominate—or indeed try to compete. Wisely, architect Robert Burley has chosen to site this house so that a high lip of rock at the top of the promontory shields the house and acts as a "railing," and so that a few trees soften the stark and beautiful views. Because of its siting, its shape, and its white cedar finish, the house is hardly visible from offshore.

While at first glance this house appears simple and subdued, it is full of visual surprises—changes of scale and heights, unexpected views, and a thoroughly pleasant plan that must be a joy to live with.

In concept, the house is a fragmented pyramid pulled apart into four cedar-shingled blocks with tall, glass-walled galleries separating each one. The pitched roofs and fragmented character bear a strong relationship, again, to the site; and the cedar shingle exterior and edge-grain fir interior give the house a quiet consistency that sets off (or is set off by) the dramatic site and architectural forms of the house. Creating this quiet simplicity requires, of course, great care and skill in detailing: note the absence of fascias at the eaves, and the walls "beveled" back to the windows without apparent thickness at the corners. On the inland side, the house is approached through heavy spruce forest and the impact of the views is not felt until one has moved well into the house.

The living spaces are thoughtfully disposed into the segments of the house. From the entry, two broad halls or galleries—both glass walled at their ends and thus offering dramatic glimpses to the forest and sea—lead to the master-bedroom suite or to the kitchen-dining pavilion. The high-ceilinged living room is entered, up four broad steps, from either gallery. Stairs in both hall wings lead to an upstairs gallery, serving a study (above the master bedroom) and a second bedroom (tucked under the roof of the kitchen-dining pavilion).

Architects: Robert Burley Associates. *Location:* the Maine coast. *Contractor:* E. L. Shea, Inc.

In section, the living room pavilion is raised above the main floor level to accommodate an immovable piece of the Maine shoreline which cropped up at that spot, and to give the large glass walls of the living room a clearer view to the sea. All photos show a skill in craftsmanship that is rare today—and both architect and owner are high in their praise for builder Phil Shea. Inside, all floors, ceilings, and walls are edge-grain fir panelling except for black Maine slate on the gallery level and in the kitchen. Shingles are white cedar; windows, and sliding doors are framed in bronze-finish aluminum. Roofs were truncated at the top to simplify framing, and these flat sections are metal-capped. Square footage of the house: 2,020.

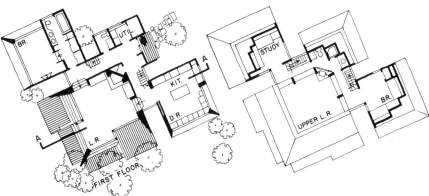

3: Houses for meadow

Meadows—broad and sometimes rolling fields—are found everywhere: in the plains, rolling down to the sea or to lakes, often high on mountainsides. Unlike beach sites, where sun and wind and sand often dictate a design solution, and unlike hillsides, where the slope almost always dictates the essential form of the house, meadowlands appear to impose few constraints. Nonetheless, while all of the 14 houses on the next 38 pages are very different—reflecting different climates, different views, different planning needs, as well as different design philosophies—there are some apparent "rules"—common design developments.

Meadow sites seem to call for a house with a strong design presence (compared, for example, to woodland houses, which seem to want to "blend in"). Thus, all but one of the houses in this chapter are two-story, and even the lone one-story house is set above its meadow on a platform. It is not a matter of reaching up for the view; most of these houses have their main living spaces on the first floors, with bedrooms on the upper level. And it is not just because two-story solutions are generally cheaper to build than a one-story house of the same size. It is more a matter of scale and proportion: on the broad canvas of a meadow site (perhaps even framed by woods or stone walls), the central theme—the house—wants to be a strong object.

Tradition—familiar forms—leads us in the direction, of course. Think of the white farmhouses and big red barns of New England. A still better image: the white complex of house and barn, perhaps shaded by a few giant trees, that you can see from miles away as you drive along the flat roads of America's Great Plains. From a distance these house/barn complexes, set as an oasis in broad green fields, have an almost sculptural quality. And that sculptural image is not lost on contemporary architects, as we shall see. To take the familiar form first:

The house on the next pages, by architects Willis Mills and Timothy Martin,

has, in its essential form, "the austere, four-square self-sufficiency of the traditional American farmhouse"—while at the same time being thoroughly contemporary. The house in Des Moines by architect John Bloodgood (page 72)—thoroughly

contemporary in materials and form—develops strong images of both a Midwestern farmhouse with silo and barn and a French farmhouse. At Sea Ranch, an

sites

extraordinarily well-planned second-house community in California, one of the models offered for sale is a barn—built with barn construction, finished in rough boards, with the main space plus attached shapes characteristic of barns around the country. (Inside, you will not be surprised to find, architects William Turnbull and Charles Moore have devised continuously changing spaces and heights that make this house an exciting place in which to be.)

And you'll find other houses in this chapter with close antecedents in the farmhouse image.

The completely contemporary version of the meadow house might best be described as sculptural in form. Again, it is the sense that a calm meadow site can appropriately accept a strong (to some, stark) house. The second house in this chapter (page 56), by Charles Gwathmey and Richard Henderson, moves in this direction; and the third house, by architect Richard Meier, is rather more than

sculptural in form—it *is* a piece of sculpture. There is little familiar in its shape or materials or in its plan or the way it works—but it is an extraordinarily beautiful house and, though it is over five years old, it is still on the very cutting edge of contemporary design.

All of the other houses in this chapter are, you will probably perceive, somewhere between the extremes of contemporary "sculptural form" and the familiar "farmhouse form." In some cases you will find familiar materials like shingles applied to the strong and popular shed-roof form, or stone from the site laid up in strongly contemporary shapes, or warm conventional materials and shapes in houses with surprising cut-outs and openings that suggest correctly the unusual and exciting forms of the rooms inside.

Two other meadow houses in this chapter form an interesting contrast worth study if you are considering a meadow site. One is architect Hugh Newell Jacobsen's elegant house on page 76—familiar in form, but full of exciting spaces. The other is architect Robert Fitzpatrick's own house, which uses materials most often seen in city skyscrapers—essentially a cube of bronze glass set out in a woodland meadow, changing color as the day proceeds and with the seasons.

What does it add up to? That in a meadow—an open, essentially flat site, surrounded by nature in a generally quiet mood—you have perhaps more design freedom than on other sites. There are fewer constraints, and thus there are more options. As these houses show, you can build on a meadow anything from a barn to a glistening piece of white sculpture. In the hands of a sensitive architect it will look as if the meadow were a frame for the house, and the house will seem "just the right thing" for that particular meadow.

Milton Weinstock photos

Wooden panels roll across the large glazed areas on the first floor (photos at top on facing page) when the owners are away; and stack neatly, below.

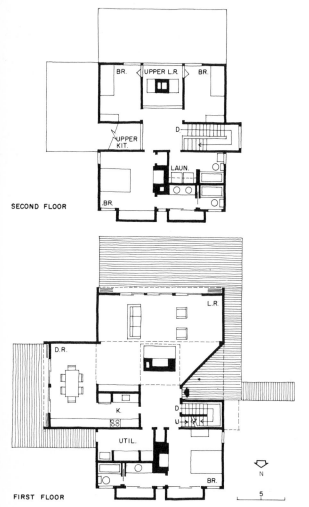

SECOND FLOOR

FIRST FLOOR

N

A CONTEMPORARY FARMHOUSE IN NEW ENGLAND

The austere, four-square self-sufficiency of the traditional American farmhouse is evoked by the exterior of this vacation house in Dublin, New Hampshire. Yet the interior, organized around the same central hall as the farmhouse, is rich in openness, informality and spatial variety.

In many ways, the problems facing those who build in northern New Hampshire have not changed in two hundred years. Therefore, the resemblance to old wood buildings is not surprising. Narrow cedar clapboards, parallel to the roof, and generous cornerboards, clearly traditional, are here used to emphasize the sweep of the two low wings away from the solid two-story main block. The diagonals at once tie the building to the land and thrust the matching half-gables to the sky.

This articulation of the gable, not to be found in old farm houses to be sure, permits a clerestory

above the second floor hall. This unexpected, almost invisible light source fills the top of the house, the stairway, the kitchen and the two-story space around the chimney with light on the dreariest day.

The living room, right, conveys the clarity of the internal organization. A substantial wood and steel truss, spanning 26 feet, supports the structure and allows the chimney of the ironspot brick fireplace to stand free in the eight-foot square space. Thus in even such an intensely planned house, one can share from the upper hall or the children's bedrooms, the activities on the lower floor.

Architects: Willis N. Mills, Jr. and Timothy Martin. *Owners:* Mr. and Mrs. Daniel Burnham. *Location:* Dublin, New Hampshire. *Structural engineer:* Paul Pantano. *Mechanical engineer:* Sanford O. Hess. *Contractor:* Bergeron Construction Co.

STRONG SHAPES AND COLORS IN A GENTLE SETTING

Excellent proof that a fresh, visually interesting building can be created within the framework of fairly stringent design codes is furnished by this handsome house. Local ordinances restricted building in the community to two-and-a-half stories in height, with a minimum of 35,000 cubic feet enclosed, and mandatory pitched roofs at not less than 6/12 slope. There were also minimum cost restrictions. Apart from the desire for a strong contemporary design, the owners' requirements were quite simple: living area, dining space, kitchen and powder room at grade level, three bedrooms and two baths above.

The white-stuccoed, terne-roofed geometric forms which evolved are probably remote from the designs the code-writers envisaged they were espousing, but following them to the letter has produced one of the most creatively significant houses of the year.

The site is a large, wooded one of 25 acres. The architects have placed the house in a private clearing within the woodland in a manner aimed at creating a series of "visual experiences". They describe it as follows: "having meandered up the winding drive, catching glimpses through the trees of the house, one arrives in a parking area. With the future addition of a garage and guest house (conceived of as a gate) the scale change from vehicular to pedestrian movement is made specific. From there, a variety of vistas, intensities and directions of light, and changes of shapes and dimensions, hopefully achieve the spatial richness and vitality we desire. Terminating the internal sequence is a complex configuration tying upper living space and stair-hall to the anchoring fireplace: here one sees back across the clearing to the enveloping woodland."

Architects: Charles Gwathmey and Richard Henderson of Gwathmey & Henderson. *Location:* Purchase, New York. *Contractor:* Caramagna, Barbagallo & La Vito. *Landscape architects and interior designers:* Gwathmey & Henderson.

MAIN FLOOR   N   5

SECOND FLOOR

Bill Maris photos

Charles Gwathmey and Richard Henderson have unified their strong architectural design in this house by planning the interiors and landscaping as well. Thus all, including the owners' harp in its special niche, has an unusual functional and visual compatibility.

As the architects stressed in their comments on the preceding page, room shapes and window placement have been studiedly varied to produce a constantly changing sequence of woodland views and lighting effects. Artificial lighting has been built-in to add yet other effects.

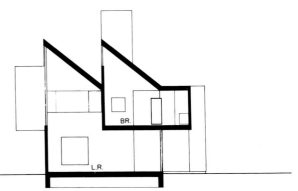

A stand of trees was the only notable site feature, and the house was oriented in part to benefit from the privacy it gives. Seemingly a purely sculptural counterpoint, the white brick chimney is in fact freestanding to permit a window above the living room mantelpiece.

PURE CONTEMPORARY SCULPTURE FRAMED BY A MEADOW

Sculptural forms, and the complex interior spaces that they express, combine to make this Long Island house a dramatic and delightful home for a young family with three active children. Presenting a blank face to the nearby road and opening to a private lawn and woodland to the rear, the neatly organized—and very comfortable—house is built of glass and white-painted wood for a great air of spaciousness.

Living areas open into each other for light and view, but the great visual interest of this house stems from its unusual plan. Rooms are organized in two diagonally-intersecting rectangles and the resulting interpenetration of colliding spaces makes looking—and especially moving—through all this house a source of constantly surprising delight. Enjoyment of a house can come from the things in it—in this house pleasure is built in.

Family and entertaining activities center on an imposing two-story living room. This is flanked by a contrasting, low-ceilinged dining area and an out-of-the-way sitting corner, and overlooked by an angled, study-playroom balcony. Varied windows shared by all include floor-to-ceiling glass on the northwest, a clerestory for morning light, and a large corner window placed over the fireplace. Such devices as a red-painted wall downstairs, and the yellow ceiling of the upstairs hall, increase spatial depth. Otherwise pure white surfaces include practical glazed ceramic tile floors, gypsum board walls and laminated plastic countertops and cabinets.

Architect: Richard Meier. *Owners:* Mr. and Mrs. David L. Hoffman. *Location:* East Hampton, New York. *Contractor:* William Lynch.

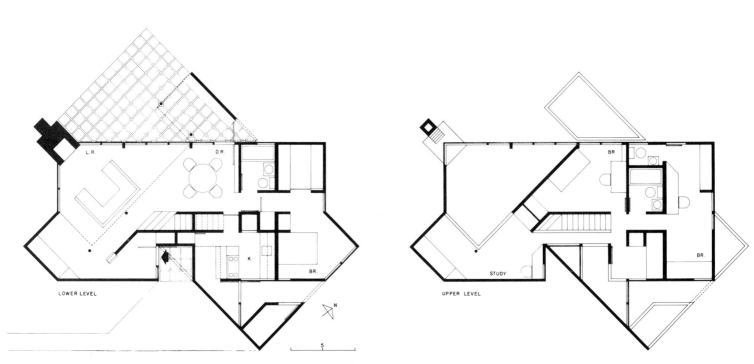

LOWER LEVEL

L.R.   D.R.

K.

BR

N

5

UPPER LEVEL

BR

STUDY

BR

Taking in a view over the skylit, two-story breakfast space, the upstairs hall of the Hoffman house doubles back to a playroom-study for a privileged outlook and shared clerestory light. The wood frame structure is supplemented by occasional steel columns, and the subfloors are plywood or concrete slab on grade.

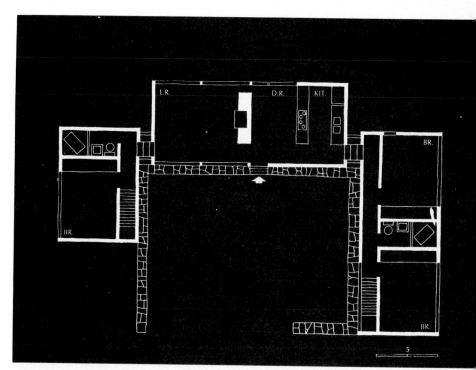

Phokion Karas photos

A CONTEMPORARY USE
OF TRADITIONAL FORMS
BY THE SEA

The shed roof—still very much a dominant theme in contemporary architecture—maintains its freshness and originality as an architectural form in this sweeping, dramatic interpretation of the motif for a vacation house in Maine. Although it is built primarily for summer use, there is provision for a full heating system and the architect anticipates that the owners will use the house for longer and longer periods of the year.

The house is sited on the crest of a hill overlooking York Harbor and is built around the stone foundations of a previous building. The living areas command a dramatic view of the water.

Complete separation of the living areas from family and guest bedrooms was a fundamental program requirement and this led Herbert Vise to develop a tripartite plan in which each part of the building is separately articulated. At first each building was planned to be physically separate from the others, but in the end, convenience demanded internal connections at either end of the living section.

The structure of all three buildings is simple wood frame with exterior walls of white cedar shingle. Wood studs and sheathing are left exposed on the interior walls, while ceilings are exposed, unfinished wood joists and boarding.

The house derives its interest from the strength of its elevations, from the architect's refusal to compromise with or attempt to soften the effects of a rugged site, and from the bold handling of roughly textured, natural materials. At night the expansive glazed areas throw the form of the building into dramatic relief.

Architect: Herbert Vise. *Owners:* Mr. and Mrs. William Harby. *Location:* York Harbor, Maine. *Contractor:* Dominic W. Gratta.

In contrast to the many architects who would define architecture as the enclosure of space, Herbert Vise says that his initial concept of a building is as a total "mass" which he then "hollows out" to meet the spatial needs of his clients and to express his own personal esthetic. Vise believes it essential that the over-all mass of the building should "complement" the site and "be identifiable with the indigenous buildings of the locale."

Vise has succeeded in giving this

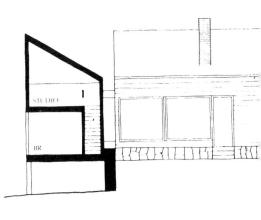

house a distinctly regional flavor which makes it right for its site and creates something of the feeling of those beautiful New England barns. The relationship of the interior to the exterior—as expressed by the dramatic window treatment—demonstrates a strongly sculptural quality.

Mr. Harby is a painter and wanted to use the house as a studio. The great sense of freedom and the uncluttered interiors make this an ideal "loft in the country."

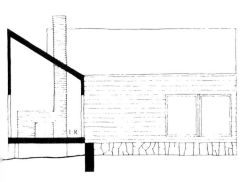

STRICT SIMPLICITY IN A WOODLAND FIELD

Chameleon-like, the reflective bronze glass walls of this elegantly wood-framed house change appearance with the seasons, and add a considerable degree of internal privacy and glare control. Architect Fitzpatrick professes that he is fascinated by small French pavilions, and he has been extremely successful here in creating a contemporary version of one using today's most modern materials and equipment.

The serene, precisely designed house is set on a grass terrace, and approached along a rising curved gravel drive to a court formed against the hillside. Views expand in all directions over meadows and woods.

Inside, the house has considerable spatial and visual interest, as well as areas of quiet and privacy. The main living area, which measures 20 by 45 feet, is two stories high at its center. Balconies overlook it on three sides and add spaces for study, art studio and a connecting gallery to display paintings by the architect. The combination of glass walls looking outward, low- and high-ceilinged areas, balconies and alcoves greatly increases the sense of spaciousness, and the usefulness of the house. The bronze glass and white color scheme of the exterior also forms the basic theme for the interiors, sparked by bright primary colors of the paintings and linen cushions on chairs and benches. Most of the furniture was specially designed for the house by the architect. The main rooms were planned for comfortable country living and for frequent entertaining.

Structurally, the house is especially noteworthy for the visual slenderness of its wood frame—an illusion created by extending the thin-edged supports inwards for the needed strength, and by insetting the floor and roof supports well behind the bronze-toned glass.

Architect and owner: Robert E. Fitzpatrick. *Location:* Yorktown, New York. *Engineers:* Tege Hermansen (structural), Douglas Gawman (mechanical). *Interior design:* Mary Fitzpatrick.

FIRST FLOOR   SECOND FLOOR   5

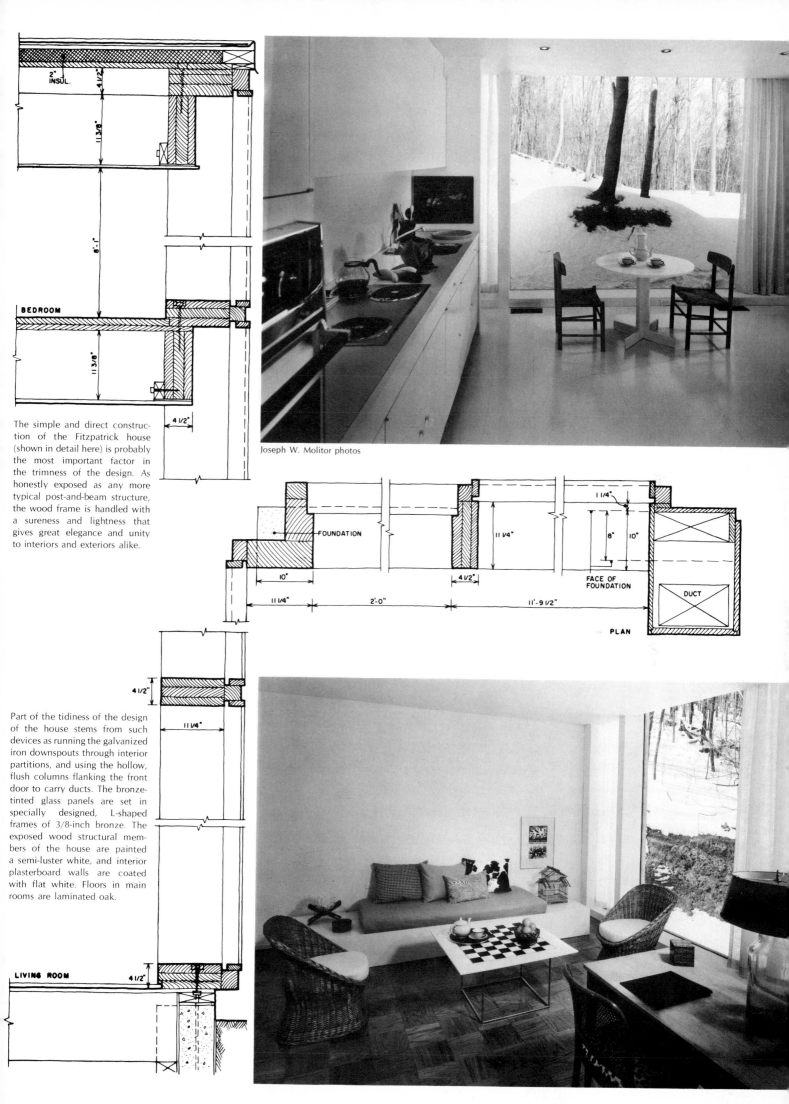

The simple and direct construction of the Fitzpatrick house (shown in detail here) is probably the most important factor in the trimness of the design. As honestly exposed as any more typical post-and-beam structure, the wood frame is handled with a sureness and lightness that gives great elegance and unity to interiors and exteriors alike.

Joseph W. Molitor photos

Part of the tidiness of the design of the house stems from such devices as running the galvanized iron downspouts through interior partitions, and using the hollow, flush columns flanking the front door to carry ducts. The bronze-tinted glass panels are set in specially designed, L-shaped frames of 3/8-inch bronze. The exposed wood structural members of the house are painted a semi-luster white, and interior plasterboard walls are coated with flat white. Floors in main rooms are laminated oak.

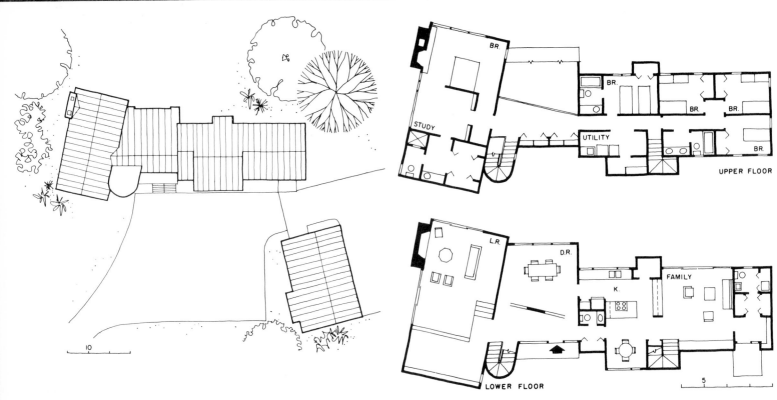

STUDY

BR.

BR.

BR.

BR.

UTILITY

BR.

UPPER FLOOR

L.R.

D.R.

FAMILY

K.

LOWER FLOOR

10

5

A MIDWESTERN FARMHOUSE IN MODERN FORM

This spirited house complex stems from the owners' rather singular desire for a house that was a "cross between an early European chateau (fortress-like rather than ornamented) and a Midwestern farmhouse."

The architect comments that "the site is a natural one for this kind of combination: the house is placed at the end of a long sloping meadow, at the edge of a wood which borders a river. Thus, the reclusive nature of the house from the approach side, and the very open nature of the other side for the view of the woods. The massing was devised to suggest an accumulation of individual structures rather than a single design monolith." The result is a very successful house that is extremely contemporary, yet *does* suggest the qualities desired.

The plan is zoned into a parents' living and sleeping wing, and a wing for the children. The arrangement of the children's rooms reflects the owners' wish to have them used for sleeping and private study only; play and other noisier activities are planned for the family room.

The forms of all these spaces are fairly vigorously expressed on the exterior, yet unified by the terne roofs, and by walls surfaced with cement plaster (broken only for expansion joints) and painted a soft cream color, as is all trim. The one accent is the bright barn red of the front door (see cover).

White-painted plasterboard walls and brick tile floors are the typical interior finish. Trim is minimal throughout. Vinyl tile floors are used in the children's wing and in the kitchen. The house has thermostatically-controlled air conditioning.

The comfortable interior furnishings were planned by the owners, and reflect the casual-formal qualities of the house.

Architect: John D. Bloodgood. *Owners:* Mr. and Mrs. Frederick Weitz. *Location:* Des Moines, Iowa. *Contractor:* The Weitz Company.

The openness of the interiors contrasts with the closed facade on the motor court. The approximate cost of the house, without lot, landscaping and furnishings, was $75,000.

Hedrich-Blessing photos

A VERY SPECIAL FORM
FOR A SEA-MARSH SETTING

Designed for a young sub-urban family, this unusual cedar-clad house located on Long Island Sound beautifully illustrates—and unites—two notable trends in contemporary house design: first, a tendency to reinstate traditional materials and vernacular forms; second, a tendency more and more sensitively to respond to the special character of the land. The resulting design is not only very practical but suited to its owners' modern needs and style. The owners' family includes three boys, and their influence was felt in the many playful aspects of the scheme, including the diverse windows which seem to climb up the roof or peer out amid the trees. The site is beautiful: an acre of meadowland on the Connecticut shore. Its greatest assets are an old oak tree some 90 feet tall and an unhindered view of the water, its sailboats in

SECTION A-A

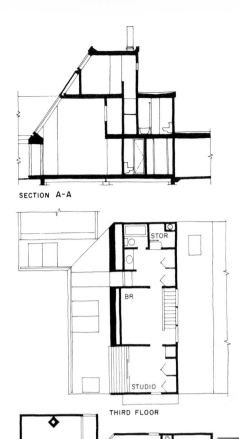

THIRD FLOOR

Marsh grass is the natural fabric of which one is most immediately aware and the house was in fact conceived as a "raft" floating on that "sea." The wall baffling the patio is curved powerfully to anchor the house to the landscape and the tree. Though it faces a field, privacy was not a problem, as the house is a division of a former estate whose development included provision for open land. The fireplace is freestanding and walls act as planes to open vistas throughout.

SECOND FLOOR

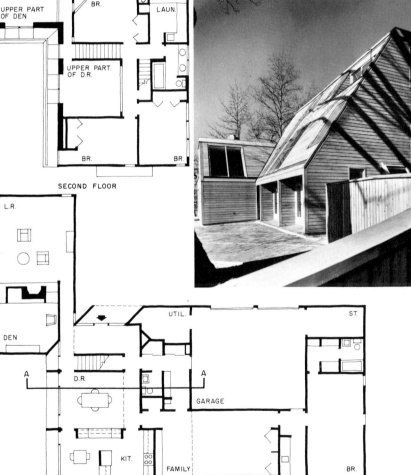

FIRST FLOOR

5

the distance and tidal flats nearby: "the design of the house literally revolves around this tree and the water view," the architects explain. Thus the orientation of major rooms, and the sizes and shapes of all the windows were determined by the views, to give the owners

maximum and varied enjoyment from various rooms: the deep window seen above opens up the stairwell; the topmost window was designed, like the forecastle of a ship, to "project" the viewer over the sea. For all its unorthodoxy, it is perhaps surprising that the most un-

usual quality of this house is the love of tradition it reflects—partly as response to the owners' requests, partly as a fitting response to its location: traditional pitched roofs and shiplapped siding are also responses to the sea. "We are traditionalists," the owners concur.

Architects: T. M. Prentice, Lo-Yi Chan and Rolf Ohlhausen of Prentice & Chan, Ohlhausen—Martha Carder, project architect. Owners: Mr. and Mrs. Peter F. McSpadden. Location: Riverside, Connecticut. Mechanical engineer: Harold Hecht & Associates. Landscape Architect: George Cushing. Contractor: Donald R. Smith, Inc.

AN ELEGANT EASTERN SHORE HOUSE

In size and scale and form and rambling shape, this house on the shores of Chesapeake Bay is reminiscent of the elegant manor houses of Maryland's Eastern Shore. But these characteristics give way under architect Hugh Jacobsen's hand to a thoroughly contemporary house that is thoughtfully and functionally zoned; dramatic (indeed sometimes spectacular) but always human in scale; full of pleasant surprises; and—very consciously—starkly contrasted against its site.

Jacobsen's essential scheme, from which everything else follows, was to divide the house into four elements, each with its own steeply pitched roof. As the plan shows, each element is a separate zone—garage/utility, kitchen/dining, entry/living room, and bedroom/library—so

positioned that every room overlooks the view, circulation is sensible and straightforward, and the handsome stone-paved entry court is formed.

The house is built of white stucco over block, with a black asphalt shingle roof set off by the parapets that sharply define the edges of each element against the sky. All of the glass—both fixed and operative—is tinted and tempered plate. Interior finishes are drywall on walls and ceiling, floors are oak except in the kitchen.

Jacobsen's attention to detail is evident everywhere: in the slit windows that permit surprise views from many rooms; in the slit skylights which give unexpected glimpses of the sky and contribute to an ever-changing quality of light; in the slender detailing of the screen porch and

window framing; in the strongly expressed rain gutters with anchor chain "down-spouts." Other examples: in the bedroom wing, pockets in the walls contain a sliding glass panel, a screen panel, and a teak louvered panel for privacy and light control.

And everywhere, inside and out, there is an absence of casings or moldings or bases or trim—an absence of detail which is the best but always the most difficult kind of detailing.

Architect: Hugh Newell Jacobsen. *Location:* Eastern Shore, Maryland. *Structural engineer:* James Madison Cutts. *Mechanical engineer:* Alexander Blumenthal. *Contractor:* Ships Point Construction Company.

Robert C. Lautman photos

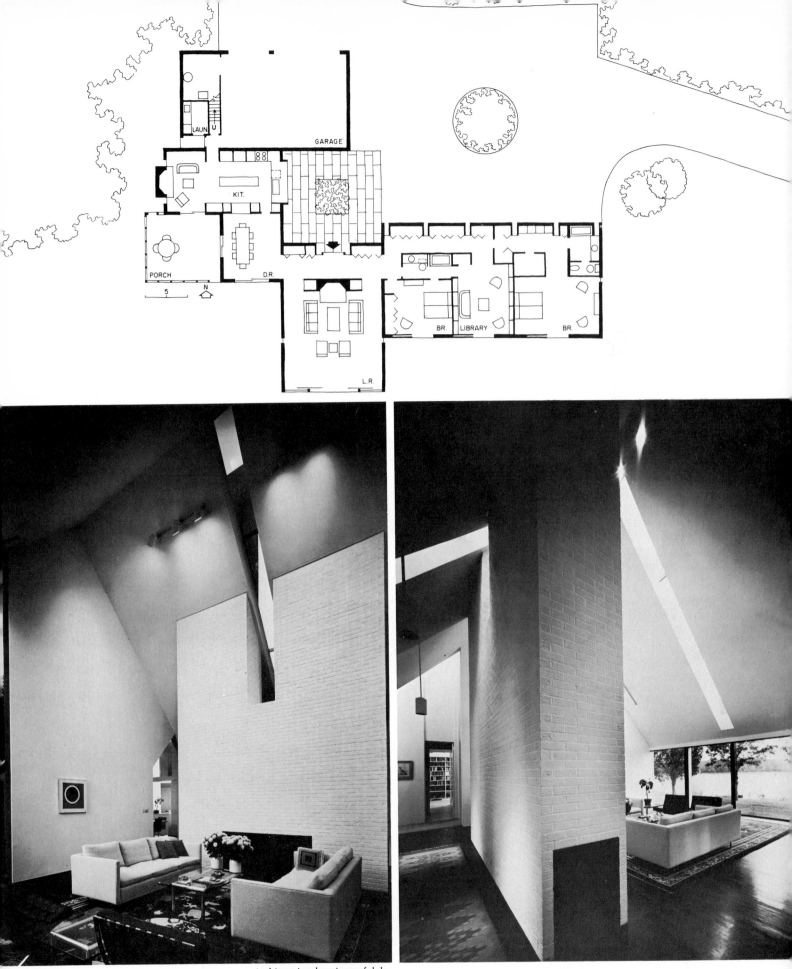

Architect Jacobsen's careful detailing is evident throughout the interiors. Ceilings follow the form of the roof, are slit by skylights. The fireplace wall separates living room from entry (above). The kitchen (opposite) has its own seating area in front of the dramatic glass-framed fireplace.

Weathered white cedar shingles and corner board windows are pure Cape Cod vernacular and picked because they make good sense. Decks (photo above) are off master bedroom; (below) off livingroom on second floor. Lower level bedroom windows peer through cedar trees close by. Entry leads to low-ceilinged hall (right), open to kitchen above, and yellow enameled cast iron spiral stair. Seemingly complex, the house was designed by juxtaposing two squares, then removing triangular volumes (for decks, pitched roof) as it goes up. House has concrete block foundation to anchor it to the ground, virtually composed of shifting sand.

FOR CAPE COD:
FAMILIAR MATERIALS, NEW FORMS

When the owners leave their suburban home on summer weekends, they retreat to this unorthodox vacation house perched atop a Cape Cod hill. "Like a ship floating on the land" is how the architect Giovanni Pasanella's associate, Thea Kramer, describes the house, and the analogy is a good one. The hilltop site is flat, and, except for sand formations, scrub pines and other hardy flora, totally undistinguished. But the views—of the sea, a salt marsh, and a distant town—are great, and varied in all directions. No building is close by. By breaking up the usual four-square box to create many viewing angles (both through and out the house), the architect reasoned that he could take best advantage of the site, while still organizing the house for the owner's practical requirement: "an economical, varied space for themselves and guests to feel

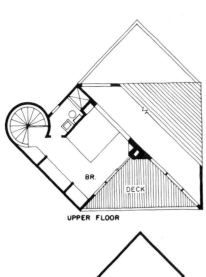

UPPER FLOOR

LOWER FLOOR

MAIN FLOOR

5

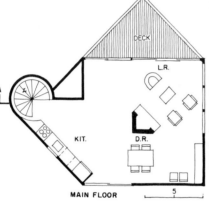

SECTION A-A

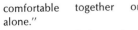

View (above) is master bedroom, overlooking living room and opening to its own deck, which, in turn, overlooks living room. Walls are cedar plywood; exposed structure is enameled a deep red. Exposed framing painted as trim helped reduce costs. Play of space is stabilized by warm red tones and the orientation the stair and fireplace provide.

David Hirsch photos

comfortable together or alone."

Spaces and shapes lend this house its perennial vacation air of built-in delight and relaxation. It is a vacation environment—though equipped with space heating and all amenities for year-round use and planned with realism.

To take best advantage of the view, the usual multi-level house plan has been reversed, with major living areas open to major views on the second floor, and children's and guest bedrooms a few steps below the first, or entry, floor. Master bedroom is on the third. By going up instead of out, and by

placing main glass areas clear of the ground, the house can be totally buttoned up; and is worry free for the owners when away.

Architect: Giovanni Pasanella—Etel Thea Kramer, associate architect. *Owners:* Dr. and Mrs. Alan Grey. *Location:* Wellfleet, Massachusetts. *Structural engineer:* Stanley Gleit. *Contractor:* Allen Jordan.

ANOTHER STRONG SCULPTURAL SHAPE BY THE OCEAN

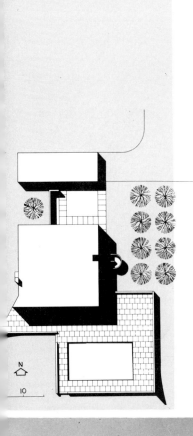

Set against the low green hills of Long Island's eastern shore, this house has a sculptural clarity that is dazzling. The Neskis, along with many other architects, are re-examining the great European work of the twenties and thirties. In this project they show that a simple square plan, strongly articulated against the sun and boldly set into nature can be powerful architecture.

Just as the jewel-like house can be seen for three or four miles from the highway, it in turn, from its relatively high spot, looks south across pastureland toward the ocean. There is nothing to give any hint of true scale. The stucco construction, carefully detailed to minimize window and door trim, presents a building whose actual size is revealed only at close range.

There are many clever devices used to make the house (just 36 feet square including the balcony) seem much larger than it is. The elevation below, facing the road, is dominated by a flying stairway from the second floor. We are used to thinking of such elements in monumental scale—five or six feet wide between railings perhaps—but here it is less than three feet wide—ample, since it is used principally to let the dog and cats out at night. The two horizontal window bands, assumed to be at eye level, actually are three to four feet above the floor (see bathroom overpage). Even the door at the right side of the facade seems taller than normal. But it isn't. Nor does either photograph of the major elevation, opposite, reveal much to the observer.

Yet if the exterior scale is a masterful illusion, the interior does not betray it either. The one large room, expressed on the exterior as glazing wrapped around the balcony, seems very spacious. Obviously, because the transparent wall fills it with light and carries the implied boundary out to the edge of the balcony and surround, if not to the horizon. The angled wall on the left side not only helps to increase the mass of the house from the exterior but substantially extends the sweeping view of the ocean from the living room.

Architects: Julian and Barbara Neski.
Owners: Mr. and Mrs. Robert Sabel.
Location: Bridgehampton, New York.

Hans Namuth photos

The stunning pair of photographs below convey the explosion of space inside the house. Carefully controlled interior details are a strong but quiet background for the rich furnishings. The bathroom, far right, is an example of careful design for which Julian and Barbara Neski are known. The exposed bulbs punched through the mirror are excellent for shaving; in the counter at the right is a flip-up mirror and separate light precisely right for makeup. Note the window above the counter.

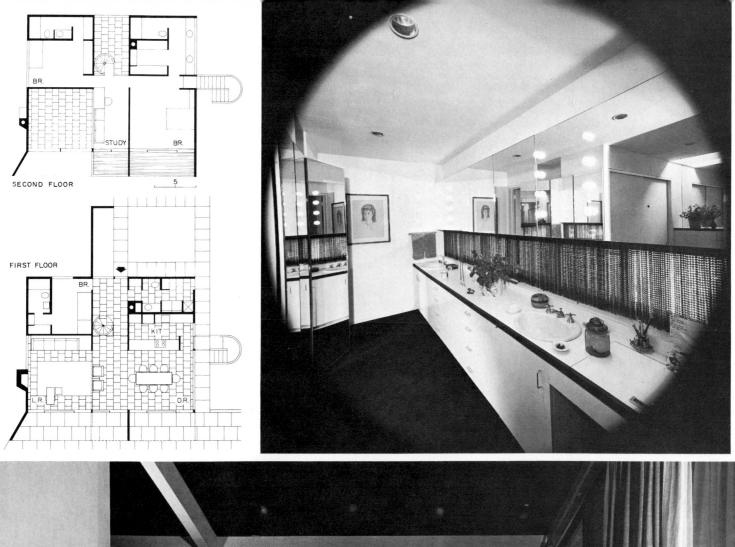

SECOND FLOOR

FIRST FLOOR

BR.

STUDY   BR.

5

BR.

KIT

L.R.   D.R.

UPPER FLOOR

MAIN FLOOR

The tall living room gives the house a spaciousness that is surprising given its size. Built-in furniture, interconnected spaces, and large windows looking into the woods in three directions also help expand the space. The section reveals a tiny, secluded roof deck reached by a ladder.

A TINY PIECE OF SUPERGRAPHICS IN A FIELD

In 1971, architect Henri Gueron built himself this three-bedroom house (including equipment, insulated, and finished interiors, as well as site work) for $15,000.

Gueron lists four ways by which he accomplished this feat: 1. Square footage was kept as low as possible, barely more than the zoning minimum of 975 square feet; 2. The house was designed on a 4- by 8-foot module, horizontally and vertically, since standard-size plywood was the ideal material for his design—both economically and esthetically; 3. Almost all prefabricated elements are also standard (the principal exception is the acrylic dome in the dining area which cost $110); 4. He served as his own general contractor for an estimated saving of 20 per cent and detailed the house to be easy to build. He estimates that done for a client using standard contract procedures, the cost would have been about $25,000.

The crisp exterior is ⅜-in. resin-impregnated plywood applied to the studs. The caulking is a white elastomeric sealant. Two coats of latex acrylic semi-gloss paint were used both on the exterior and on the drywall interiors. Finally, the bright accent colors of epoxy enamel were added. Placed diagonally on a long narrow lot studded with the scrub oak typical of eastern Long Island, the house is invisible from the road in summer but during the gray winter provides a brilliant flash of color for passers-by.

Architect and *owner:* Henri Gueron of Gueron and Lepp. *Location:* East Hampton, New York. *Engineer:* Ken Smith (electrical).

Ben Schnall photos

TION A-A

L.R.   BR.

KIT.

MOST FAMILIAR OF MEADOW SHAPES: THE BARN

A. Youngmeister photos

This ingenious vacation house has been built well over a dozen times at the Sea Ranch in California. The basic notion is simplicity itself: a barn-like space with a plan that can be flipped and with an appended lean-to whose function is variable. The working out of the notion, though, assures that simplicity does not lead to dullness.

The ground floor plan is circuitous, so that the apparent size of the space is increased because the eye can never see all of it at once. The "Z" shaped plan of the second floor allows sunlight to fall into the living areas from skylights in the roof, casting patterns that change with the hours and the seasons. It also provides upward vistas from below, and the pleasure of moving from a low space, like the dining area, to one that is dramatically higher. One can also move outside the enclosing walls of the house to lounge in a bay window, or right up to the peak of the roof to doze or sleep in one of the lofts there. What begins, then, as a simple space ends up providing an admirable array of different places to be and things to do.

The architects assumed that in a vacation house choices of what to do and where to do it would be made casually, and so the feeling of the interior is relaxed. The details are simple, the rough-sawn boards are left unfinished, and the heavy framing members stand fully exposed.

Outside, this way of building produces an effect that is downright modest, recalling simple rural structures. It has turned out that, at the Sea Ranch, this assumption of modesty was wise, for as more and more houses are built on the open meadows, each more obviously "designed" than the next, and each one competing with all the others for attention, there is the danger that the place may begin to look more like a statuary farm than the beautifully desolate landscape which it once was, and which the original developers, planners and architects had sought with great care to preserve.

Architects: William Turnbull and Charles Moore of MLTW/Moore-Turnbull—Robert Theel, associate. Location:The Sea Ranch, California. Engineers: Patrick Morreau (structural); Brelje and Race (civil). Contractor: Matthew D. Sylvia.

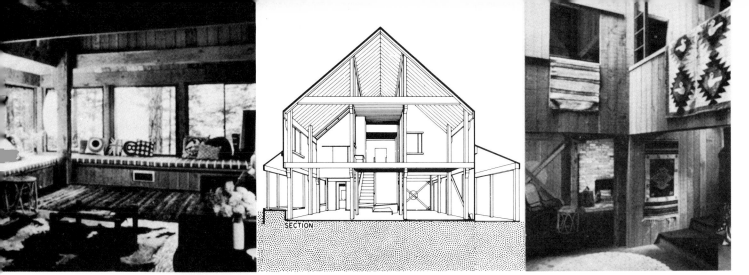

SECTION

OPEN
LOFT

LOFT

LOFT

BR   OPEN

D

OPEN   BR

SECOND FLOOR

BR

KIT

D.R

L.R

FIRST FLOOR   5

Louis Reens photos

Despite its exposed site, the Palmer house is equipped for comfort and convenience. Spaces are amply heated by two oil furnaces, one for radiant panels recessed in living room floor, and the other for convectors throughout. Foam-glass and built-up roofing provide insulation. The structure, wood frame with 14-inch-thick stone bearing walls, has a concrete block foundation. Both stone and redwood beams are exposed inside. White plaster for wood stud partitions is carried directly to beams, recalling interiors of typical Pennsylvania Dutch farmhouses.

STONE AND WOOD FOR A PENNSYLVANIA SITE

Stone and wood were the owners' requirements for their rural home perched atop a hill in the rolling farmlands of Pennsylvania Dutch country. Both materials are aptly suited to the casual living and practical wear-and-tear of an active family of six. And the rugged local fieldstone, typical of traditional Pennsylvania Dutch country buildings, is teamed with massive contemporary shed-roof forms in a merger of material and shape that reflects the stalwart character of the rustic hilltop site. Thick masonry walls and volumes give defense from a windy exposure. But the house is designed with glass and openness, as well as stone and shelter, in mind. Large expanses of floor-to-ceiling glass are open to rolling farmland, while nearby snatches of woodland view are caught by tall, slit windows. Interior sliding doors, lining living areas, open onto the sheltered two-story terrace seen in the photo above, which, with its quiet pool and slate floor, forms a transition from inside to outdoor scale. This room, measuring 23 by 23 feet, is a hub for summer family living, and, in bad weather, its blank wall forms a windbreak for the glass expanses within and frames the landscape view. The house is large, with 3500 square feet of living space.

Architect: Alfred E. De Vido. *Owner:* Mr. and Mrs. Peter Palmer. *Location:* Dallastown, Pennsylvania. *Contractor:* Robert Dunbar.

A practical four-square plan divides child and adult activities into opposite two-story quarters. The living areas of each give on to the outdoor family room, whose interior is shown at right. A master bedroom loft projects into the living room to share its light and view, and creates a quiet, darker living space beneath that contrasts with the adjacent two-story spaces (photo below). Extra light is gained upstairs by a recessed terrace and clerestories over bath and playroom. A corner kitchen is strategically placed near the entry, recreation room and maid's quarters. Five baths and ample storage space are included. The recessed entry links with a central stair in a quick circulation scheme that completes the compact plan.

PLOT PLAN

UPPER LEVEL

1 Open to living
2 Master bedroom
3 Guest bedroom
4 Terrace
5 Children's bedroom
6 Children's living room

1 Living room
2 Dining room
3 Kitchen
4 To utility—storage
5 Entry
6 Maid's quarters
7 Recreation room
8 Outdoor room

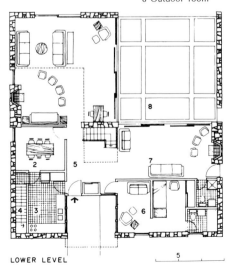

LOWER LEVEL

A SIMPLE BOX RAISED ABOVE A STONY MEADOW

The use of double cantilevers from the four corners of the fieldstone base gives this house the appearance of floating over its rocky, wooded site. In addition to adapting the house uncommonly well to the irregularities of the terrain, this device was a major design consideration to minimize any "earthbound" feeling of the owner, who is confined to a wheelchair. Ramps, planned dimensions to accommodate easy access to all areas, and a series of contained decks for outdoor living were all carefully designed to facilitate the wheelchair's use. All major rooms open to decks and have floor-to-ceiling sliding windows to increase the sense of space.

The house is visually anchored to the site by the garage structure, which is the same rough stone as the house foundation. Wood studs and joists are used to frame the house, which is surfaced with stained cedar. The house is fully air conditioned, with ducts run through the partial basement and crawl space to floor registers along all glass areas.

Architect: Herbert Beckhard. *Owners:* Mr. and Mrs. George Reed. *Location:* Danbury, Connecticut. *Interior design:* Herbert Beckhard. *Contractor:* Lester Havens.

Ben Schnall photos

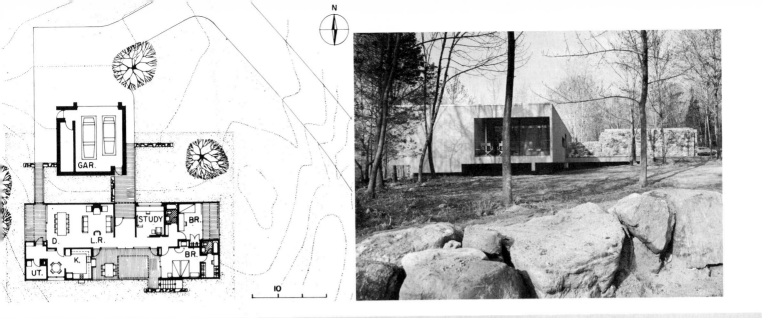

4: Houses for sites in the

This is a very common design problem, for there are woodlands everywhere. Such sites are, of course, more varied than beach sites—and thus "the rules" for woodland houses are broader and more subjective.

But even though the 10 houses in this chapter are completely varied—from sort-of-rustic to super-sophisticated—there are common characteristics.

For most woodland sights, the view tends not to be as focused as it is on a beach or a mountainside. Thus the plan of woodland houses tends to be less focused. Typically, the living room does overlook the best view—whether it is a brook, or an especially handsome rock outcropping, or an especially beautiful tree or grove of trees. But the other rooms often have the same (or similarly handsome) views, and thus a sensitive design can create varied and sometimes surprising views from each room. The entry side is typically used as the service side, overlooking the road and driveway, with necessary areas for garbage and fuel storage, and for the garage.

If the site is so wooded as to be dark despite judicious clearing, light can be let into the house in dramatic ways. Thus, in woodland houses, we frequently see skylights or clerestories, or light scoops that capture light at rooftop (and treetop) level and funnel it through the house. For the same reason, sundecks or solariums on the upper levels or roof of a woodland house can sometimes offer welcome spots for sunny relaxation—together with an exciting "tree-house" view.

What about clearing? With our increased awareness of conservation and ecology, it has become rather unfashionable to cut trees. More than a few architects brag that "in the construction of this house, not a single tree was disturbed." But this attitude can be overdone. Surely a house should be sited to spare magnificent trees, but, equally surely, modest clearing to free up a floor plan or to open a view is appropriate. Further, in many long-wild sites, clearing unhealthy trees and "junk" trees, and even some good trees, enables the best trees to fill out and grow stronger and more beautiful.

The problem of heavy shade again suggests care in the design of landscaping. Unless there is a sunny clearing where grass will grow well, why bother? A planting of evergreens and woodland flowering plants—with a ground cover of myrtle or pachysandra—will be more appropriate, easier to tend, and almost surely more successful.

Just as there is a suitable vocabulary of materials for a beach house, some materials just seem more appropriate than others in a woodland site. Though you will find—and beautiful they are—two stark white houses in this chapter (one is stucco, the other white painted siding and concrete block), natural finishes seem to work better on most wooded sites. Thus on the houses in this collection we find shingles naturally finished, stained siding applied horizontally or vertically. If

woods

there's a good stone mason left in the area, using stone from the site in foundations and fireplaces is particularly appropriate and handsome. Pole houses—echoing in their basic framing the form of the trees outside—are suitable, and often make possible building on a site with dubious foundation conditions.

What plan-shapes are suggested on wooded sites? While a hundred thousand merchant builders disagree, formal Colonial plans seem singularly inappropriate in a wood. The true Colonial houses almost always sat on cleared lawns, with a degree of formality or at least order. A woodland suggests a less formal scheme. In the absence of a strong focal point on the site, rambling plans—giving each section of the house a slightly different viewpoint—make sense. Sometimes a house can be built as a "cottage colony" of separate rooms, giving a vitality to the house that suits the serenity outside. Don't assume that every room has to have a broad view. If there's a superb evergreen on the site, perhaps the best view from some room in the house could be from a tall, narrow strip window focusing just on that tree—almost as if it were a mural on the wall. And don't forget upward views—a skylight that gives you a view from bed, first thing each morning, of sunlit leaves can be far more rewarding than a sliding-glass door to nothing special.

In finishing a house, there's a tendency, with a woodland site, to "go rustic." As in a beach house, exposed framing is appropriate, but often a doubtful saving. More common—since woodland houses are not as often "summer-only" as beach houses—is heavy use of "barn lumber," rough-sawn board-and-batten finishes, stone in massive fireplaces, or, if such materials are not available, lots of plywood paneling in the multitude of natural-wood finishes on the market. Maybe it's too personal a view, but this "natural finish" idea can go too far. Wood is of course the most beautiful of materials, but an all-wood room can be too much—too much texture, too much "warmth," and just plain too dark. Similarly, a stone fireplace is, of course, one of the most beautiful and most coveted things in a house—but an overscale stone fireplace can be, again, too much. Both stone and wood paneling are often more beautiful if set off in walls of white drywall, or set under a white ceiling. "Too rustic" is as bad as "too sophisticated"—a balance of natural materials with modern materials (white walls, great sheets of glass) is often the best solution.

At any rate, the 10 houses in this chapter will give you a broad view of the design of a woodland house in the hands of 10 very skillful architects. The variety of houses will indicate that, while some attempt has been made to set down rules in this chapter introduction, there are no rules that really count. What counts is what the owner really wants—and the skill of an architect to create it.

Philip Molten photos

A SMALL BUT CAREFULLY DETAILED WOODLAND HOUSE

Within the simplest imaginable structural framework of this small (under 1,000 square feet) house, architect J. Alexander Riley has created an extraordinary variety of indoor and outdoor spaces. Essentially, as is best seen in the plan and photo at right, the house is made of two flatroofed units set seven feet apart and bridged by a handsomely framed pitched roof set above twin clerestories that pour light into the center of the house, even though it is on a northeastern slope.

That roof is one of four elements that give distinction and interest to what—in less sensitive hands—could have been quite ordinary. The second design device was staggering the ends of the elements—on both the entry and view ends of the plan—to eliminate any sense of boxiness. Third: dropping the living room floor three steps, and leaving it open to the dining room and kitchen to add a sense of spaciousness. Finally, while the house is of the simplest construction, with posts, single-thickness walls of 2¼- by 6-inch cedar and a single-thickness 2 by 6 cedar roof—great attention was paid to the detailing. Note for example the mitered corners of the clerestory structure (photo right) and the simple-to-fabricate but effective detailing of the interior (photos next page).

Architect and owner: J. Alexander Riley. Location: Inverness, California. Contractor: Jean Madill Burroughs.

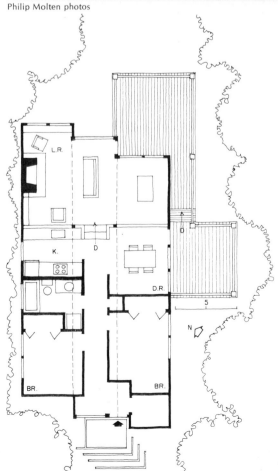

On the interiors, the simple wood framing is clearly expressed, with a small but effective amount of trim and special detailing. The photo (far right) shows the main view wall, with the deck beyond. At right, a view from the living room to the dining room and kitchen three steps above. The kitchen-living room, photo below, emphasizes the changes in scale and room shape worked out within, again, an essentially simple framework.

A HOUSE AT ONCE MODEST AND MEMORABLE

This house for an architect and his family manifests common sense as well as talent, clear sightedness as well as imagination, practicality as well as dreams. The result is modest, clear and memorable—though it may take some readjustment of our expectations to perceive it, for what we are likely to remember is not an elegant architectural effect here or a striking detail there, or indeed even some dazzling form of the whole. What we will remember is a place made simply of simple materials, well-formed around the needs of the people who live there and attentive to the land on which it is built.

These qualities are not uncommon ideals in house design, and in fact most people would call them downright basic. In practice, though, they can easily get lost in the rush to achieve other more dazzling goals.

Architect and owner: Murray Whisnant. *Location:* Charlotte, North Carolina. *Engineers:* R. V. Wasdell & Associates (structural); J. M. McDowell & Associates (mechanical); S. T. Hocsak & Associates (electrical). *Contractor:* G. E. Vinroot Construction Company.

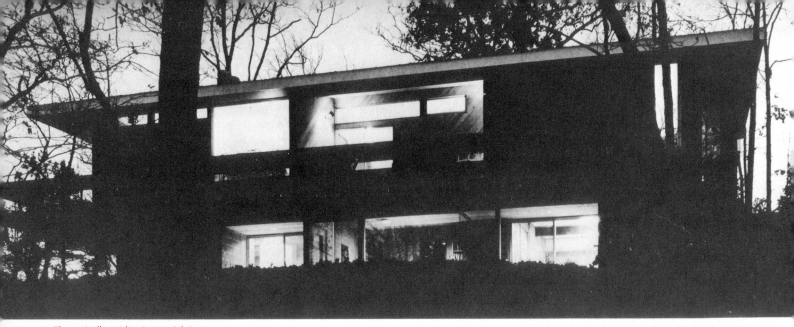

The main floor (drawing at right) is a series of rooms clustered around a central mechanical core that contains the kitchen and two baths. At one end of the plan are three bedrooms and at the other a large living and dining room that opens onto a cantilevered deck (large photo above); in front of the mechanical core is the entrance hall and behind is a small porch reached from either the master bedroom or the kitchen. On the lower level are an office (photo below right), a studio and a playroom.

The configuration of the suburban site and the placement of the buildings next door suggested that the house be relatively closed and viewless on the front and on one end (left photo below); accordingly the living room is lit on the front by a narrow band of windows just above eye level and by a sloping skylight in the ceiling (large photo opposite). At the back of the house (right photo below) the walls open up to provide a view down a wooded hill, both from the back porch and the living and dining room, and from the office below.

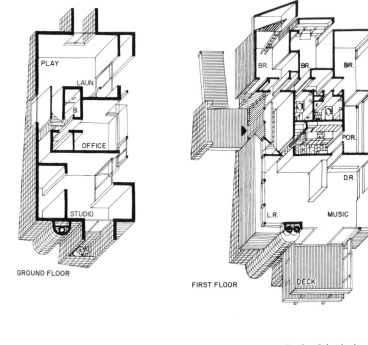

GROUND FLOOR

FIRST FLOOR

Gordon Schenk photos

A SERENE RETREAT IN THE WOODS

This serene, comfortable house was specifically planned as a secluded, informal and easy-to-keep retreat from weekdays in a New York City apartment. The site is about 100 miles from the city in a wooded area with four-acre minimum tracts, which helps assure privacy and quiet.

The plan of the house divides two sleeping areas, for owners and for guests, with a living, dining and kitchen zone. All bedrooms have large floor-to-ceiling glass areas opening to small decks at the ends of the house. The living areas have a large deck to expand the spaces for entertaining. All materials were chosen for easy maintenance for, as Herbert Beckhard observes, "heavy housekeeping chores after exposure to 100 miles of weekend traffic would be intolerable for a two or three day stay." The structure of the house uses exposed laminated columns and beams, and is sheathed with vertical and diagonal cyress siding. Interior walls are cypress or gypsum board; floors are bluestone or carpet.

Architect: Herbert Beckhard. *Owner:* Mr. and Mrs. Arnold Rosenberg. *Location:* East Hampton, Long Island, New York. *Interior design:* Herbert Beckhard. *Contractor:* Frank Johnson.

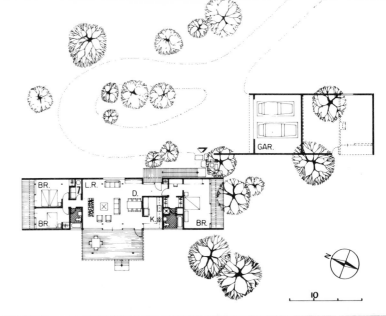

Joseph W. Molitor photos

Gil Amiaga photos

STUDIO
LOFT
UPPER L. R.
BR.
SECOND FLOOR

K
L. R.
D. R.
FIRST FLOOR
10

STRONG GEOMETRIC SHAPES AMIDST SHADOW AND SHADE

In this weekend and vacation house, architect Richard Moger displays as much skill in creating distinctive architecture with minimal size and budget as he has previously shown with more ample resources.

Though the house itself contains only 1500 square feet, and was built for $35,000, an illusion of far greater size—even luxury—has been created by some intriguing design techniques. The most obvious ones are the use of a modified "open plan," and the allocation of the greater part of the house to a big living room and minimal (but ample) spaces for other areas. These ideas, of course, have been around for quite a while, but here they have been combined with a highly successful interplay of scale,

light, openness and seclusion, which gives the sense of variety so often tragically lacking in a small house. In addition, Moger has incorporated an eye-catching *leitmotif* of rectangles and curves, all tied together by highly accented diagonal focal points; this, in the best sense, is the "decorative" element in the house—very simple, very architectural, with no frills, fuss or ostentation—and is obvious in the structure, the furnishings, even the wall hangings. This visual use of the diagonal (as can readily be seen in the photographs) increases the perspective and sense of visual space to a remarkable degree.

Though, when all doors are open, one can see—or at least be conscious of—most all of the spaces in the house

(and all these spaces somehow take advantage of the big, east-facing glass wall of the living area), necessary privacy is assured by doors to bedroom, baths, kitchen, and tracks provided for curtains, if they are desired, at the windows.

In part, the budget was met by simple construction: a wood frame on concrete block foundation, cedar siding, painted gypsum board intetiors, built-up roof, quarry tile floors, furnace in outside-access crawl space. All is neat, easy to maintain.

Architect and owner: Richard R. Moger. *Location:* Southampton, New York. *Engineers:* Langer & Polise (mechanical); Paul Gugliotta (structural). *Contractor:* John Caramagna.

Basically rectangular in shape, the house gains character by some simply achieved, but highly rhythmical undulations of walls to express the activity areas and functions occurring inside. The combined sense of shelter and openness that occurs within is also expressed in the relatively closed entrance facade (across-page), the glass at back (far left and below).

Details throughout are simple, unobtrusive, well proportioned, with spaces and massing given importance; even on a limited budget, there is no deference to the "expose all the working innards" school—the mechanics of the house are not seen.

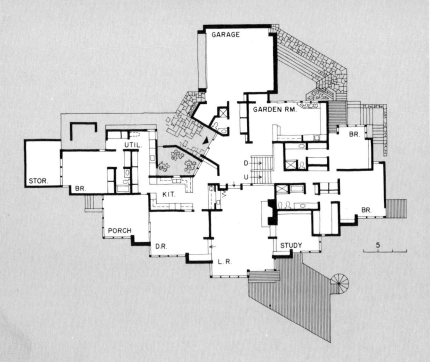

LIGHT ENTERS EVERYWHERE IN THIS SHADED HOUSE

Along a narrow shelf on this sloping, 30-acre site in central Connecticut, architect Joseph Salerno designed a new house for clients who had lived on this same property for nearly three decades. The new house is sited just to the north of the earlier residence and overlooks a small river that forms the property's northern border. A natural growth of oak and laurel enriches the gentle hillside.

During their travels, owners Mr. and Mrs. Saul Poliak have acquired a modest but carefully selected collection of paintings and art objects for which Salerno has provided a splendid background. They also share a love for plants and required a "garden room" equipped with a potting bench,

sink, and plant display areas. In other respects, the client's program was more or less orthodox.

Because the major rooms were oriented to the north, Salerno tilted the roof plane, or sections of it, to bring sunlight from the south deep into the interiors. Even on overcast days, the living and dining areas are flooded with reflected light. The interior spaces are loosely defined, giving way to each other in interesting spatial patterns. The living room is dominated by a massive masonry fireplace laid up in stones collected from the property. The same stone is used selectively for structure in the house and for retaining walls outside. Other building and finish materials include redwood

for exterior walls, gypsum board on interior partitions, wood parquet for floors and aluminum sash on windows and sliding door assemblies. A redwood deck (photos opposite, middle and above) stretches out over the falling contours to offer a splendid view of river and trees.

The Wrightian echoes—both in massing and in window details—seem welcome and adroitly handled.

Architect: Joseph Salerno (Audrey Greenwald, project architect). Owners: Mr. & Mrs. Saul Poliak. Location: West Redding, Connecticut. Engineers: Viggo Bonnesen & Associates (structural); John L. Altieri (mechanical/electrical). Interior design consultant: Betty Cavallon. Landscape architect: Evan Harding. Contractor: Joseph A. Marino.

Pedro E. Guerrero photos

The owners anticipate using the foundations of their old residence—just south of the present site—to create a multi-level garden. The "planned" character of the garden will make a nice contrast to the natural growth on the slope toward the river.

A TALL SHINGLE HOUSE
IN A CALIFORNIA GROVE

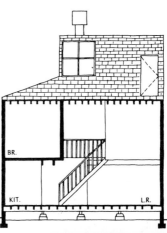

A three-story-high vertical living space transforms this simple-appearing, shingle-clad house into quarters for a very relaxed way of life. The architects state that "the owners had tired of their large conventional house, and were anxious to spend their limited budget on the excitement usually associated with a vacation house, rather than on the fixtures and appliances ordinarily expected in a house for year-round living." The resulting house thus minimizes "service" aspects (there is a wall-kitchen), and concentrates on a riot of color, space, comfort, books, music, and a balcony which serves as a quiet sitting nook, and occasionally as a stage for theatricals and a place to hold a band for parties.

The owners, Mr. and Mrs. Karas, are a couple whose children are grown. Thus "zoning" was not as important as in a house for a larger family; living space, in effect runs throughout the house, wheeling around the little service core on the first floor, and rising to the high shed roof. There are two principal bedrooms and a bath on the second level; on the third level is a loft, reached by a ladder, for visiting children.

Architects: Charles W. Moore and William Turnbull, Jr. of MLTW/Moore Turnbull. *Owners:* Mr. and Mrs. Sam Karas. *Location:* Berkeley, California. *Engineer:* Patrick Morreau of Davis & Morreau Associated; *Contractor:* Douglas S. Chandler.

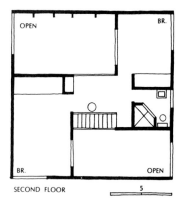

SECOND FLOOR   5

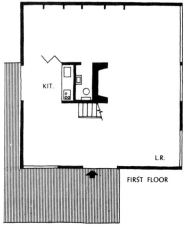

KIT.

L.R.

FIRST FLOOR

A "sun scoop" is employed in the Karas house to gain extra light on the pine-forested site, which is often foggy and sunless. Over one of the larger, upper windows in the living space, a "white baffle with an enormous yellow sun painted on it is enlisted to bounce south light into the house and to warm up the atmosphere within to a surprising degree", according to the architects.

A lower-ceilinged portion of the first floor living area is dominated by a large fireplace, which was cast in sand on the floor of the house by the contractor. This area has been treated as a smaller, cozier retreat, as contrasted with the taller reaches of other parts of the room. The furnishings of the house, many of which are built-in, are simple and sturdy, and rely for effect on bright splashes of color and a liberal sprinkling of handcraft accessories. As its original program has intended, the house does lend itself to a sort of perpetual vacation life—and in a remarkable and very different way.

AN ALL-WOOD HOUSE IN THE WOODS

*This Ohio house solves an unusual site problem
in a romantic but straightforward way
by blending a 19th century building technique
with 20th century planning concepts.*

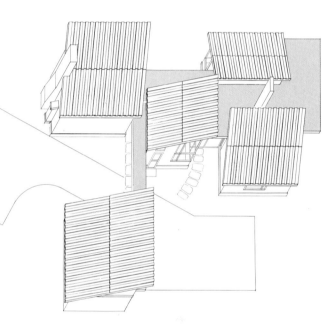

C. W. Ackerman photos except as noted

Many architects are exploring vernacular forms and techniques in houses today as a means of re-humanizing the built environment. But if the designer does not logically relate these forms and techniques to site and program, the building loses architectural clarity and integrity. It is subject to the same excesses as badly-done Georgian, Cape Cod or whatever style. It is the strong relationship between site, program and building technique that makes this house in Painesville, Ohio, by architect William B. Morris, noteworthy.

The two acres of land on the Grand River in a completely built-up neighborhood near the center of town had long been bypassed. The flat part of the site, covered with large conifers, lay 30 feet below the road (and 40 feet above the river). Rather than try to build on the unstable hillside near the road, Morris chose to place the house on the flat land, below, and designed a gentle drive notched into the hillside which returns on itself to end in the midst of the house. Faced with the problem of a one-story house approached from above,

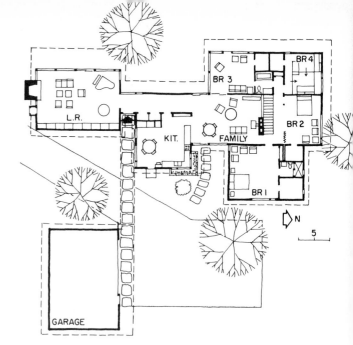

Erol Akyavas

the architect has juxtaposed shed roofs over the garage and important rooms in the house with the flat roof above circulation space and other minor rooms. The sloping roofs are roll roofing under 1 x 12 rough cedar siding laid board on board and nailed to furring strips. This technique was often used on 19th century Ohio farm buildings.

What appears then to be a well-composed collection of rural utility structures—a "village of forms"—is in fact a well-zoned, spacious house. The plan has all the functional advantages of the mid-20th century ranch-style house while relating to the site in an imaginative and appropriate way. At the time the house was designed, the Lintern family included five adolescents. This fact shaped the planning process in several interesting ways. First, provision was made for a family room, the children's living room, that was well separated from the parents' living room. Second, two of the four bedrooms were designed for other uses in the future. Bedroom 2, which is separated by a movable wall from the family room, will become Mr. Lintern's study and bedroom 3 will become a screened porch.

Finally, the owners saw the building of the house as a cultural experience for children who had grown up in a 150-year-old farmhouse. In fact, the four Lintern sons actively assisted master builder Jim Fahnestock (the only sub-contractor was an Amish mason) throughout the building process.

Architect: William B. Morris. Owner: Mr. and Mrs. James Lintern. Location: Painesville, Ohio. Engineers: Ed Amos (structural), Denk-Kish (mechanical). Lighting consultant: Lloyd Amster. General contractor: James C. Fahnestock.

Erol Akyavas

Having enjoyed the play of forms visible from the curving approach road, visitors drive past tall pines and under a low, steel-framed breezeway (left) which connects the garage and the main entrance (above). This structural tour-de-force is a well-scaled clue to the sophistication that the house has so far effectively hidden under its board roofs. The tall kitchen window (right) dominates the informal courtyard while the living room above and other areas focus on the view toward the river. The fireplace burns logs standing on end.

Erol Akyavas

Rough-sawn cedar 1 x 12s, applied board on board as siding as well as roofing, run from brick base to the 6 x 16 Douglas fir beams (left). Standard wood casement windows have been neatly integrated into the siding (below). The butternut wood cabinets separating the kitchen from the family room (bottom) were built on the job. Unpunched roofing slate was used for the entry floor.

William B. Morris

Rondal Partridge photos

A STRONG WHITE SHAPE IN THE WOODS

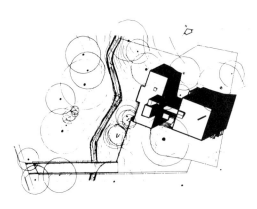

A good site can be a great asset in designing a house and, like a restricted budget, a challenge as well. In this case, the site is a small but a very romantic and private one in Berkeley, California—a wooded lot on the slope of a creek, accessible only by a long bridge. Instead of blending the structure with the woods, architect Donald Olsen has offset—and enhanced—the setting with an uncluttered geometry, equally uncluttered spaces, and a sophisticated choice and handling of major exterior materials: stucco, glass and black aluminum trim. Elegant detailing and expansive spaces were achieved within the discipline of simple wood framing and an unusually practical plan. Deliberately varied living areas are as strikingly responsive to the potential of the site as the deliberately simple form.

Architect: Donald E. Olsen. *Owners:* Mr. and Mrs. Herman D. Ruth. *Location:* Berkeley, California. *Engineer:* Jack N. Kositsky. *Landscape architect:* Peter Walker, Sasaki, Walker & Associates. *Contractor:* Charles Mee.

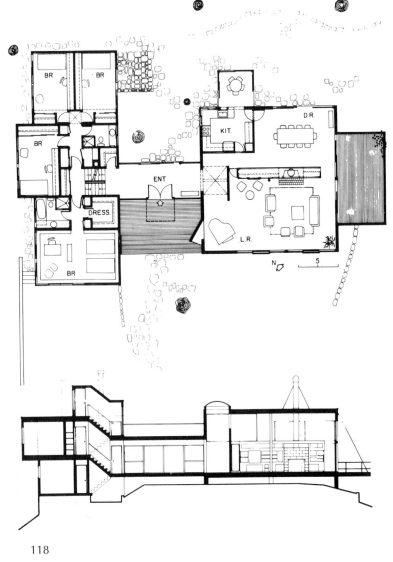

The living pavilion shown on these pages is only 32 feet square but gives the impression of being twice that size. Cabinets, shelves and fireplace are pulled together in a central divider to baffle living and dining areas and leave the perimeter free for glass. Though monochromatic, the house was in fact designed to support bright color, which comes from a yellow rug, red wall tapestry and the large-scale paintings the owners collect.

A separation of activities, as well as space for entertaining, was required. Minimal vertical traveling was another major request. Technically, the preservation of the site of several very large oak trees proved the most demanding problem, influencing not only the shape and orientation of the house, but the construction of a foundation made of special shallow-grade beams. A two unit plan admirably exploits the natural slope and views while meeting practical needs.

In addition to the bedrooms shown in the ground level plan, the second tighter unit makes use of the slope to dispose a t.v. room on the lower level, with a small, roof-level "penthouse" on the third floor. The owners are delighted with their house. "This house *is* light" they report, and natural light from varied sources does form a major design ingredient, combining with recessed fluorescent lighting and white walls.

The dining room is part of the living pavilion shown on the preceding page. Floors are oak strip. Black anodized aluminum is used for sliding doors. "It's a house that's comfortable with our modern furniture," said the client, "but I'm sure that if someone moved in with Louis XV it would look just as well." The site is a small division of a 50-year-old estate designed by Frederick Law Olmsted to provide color throughout the year, and care was taken not only to preserve the huge trees but to return the land, which abounds in rhododendrons, camellias and fuchsias, to its early, "natural" state. A virtual umbrella over the house was created through its careful placement among the trees. Because of this measure, no air conditioning was required. The view, below right, is from the living unit through to the entrance hall. Many vistas and changing shadow patterns add visual interest throughout. The entrance hall gives directly onto the rear terrace, right, to facilitate entertaining outdoors. Everywhere possible opportunity is taken to expand the visual space, but there is plenty of opportunity for privacy as well. A penthouse, shown at right, was designed as "an elevated version of a conversation pit" and gets a view past branches of the trees.

Morley Baer photos, by courtesy of House & Garden

IN CALIFORNIA: A CONTEMPORARY BARN

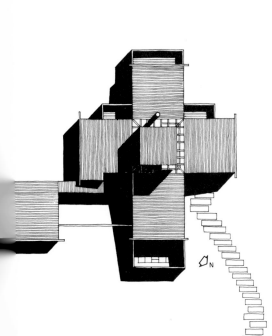

⏀N

Vertical siding, shed roofs, cantilevered decks, and, especially, the turret-like lookout room—all elements of the house shown on these pages are in the current idiom. But this "sophisticated American barn" goes far beyond the merely fashionable, exuberantly exploiting the possibilities of its oak-tree-shaded, hilltop site, while gearing itself to both the general and special needs of the clients' program. The house, designed by architects Robert Fisher and Rodney Friedman, is located in a California land subdivision, placed on a sharp ridge and a less-than-an-acre lot. Going two stories high to overlook mountains and valleys to the west and north, it has a cross-shaped plan to give unusual and varied exposure to the surroundings. And it is strategically positioned to create outdoor living spaces under the 60-foot-wide live oaks which have been left on the site. By cantilevering bay window, decks, and the house itself out over the edge of the slope, the architects were able to set the structure well back from the street, add living space to the interior and add drama to the view. While the house does look outward, it focuses inward on itself too, centering on a clerestoried gallery topped by an aerie-like second-level tower seen above. Special kinds of materials, finishes, spaces and objects are used to give special character to every room. The outline of the plan shown at left and the rustic exterior belie the excitement that the house reserves for the interior, which makes its own intriguing environment in close relationship to the outdoors.

The studio loft is reached by a steel and oak spiral stair from the gallery. Stained glass used for the entrance is an old church window. Delight is taken in the decorative quality of even common objects: note the old-fashioned ceiling fan in the loft. The garage, shown in plan, is placed to baffle the dining terrace from neighbors.

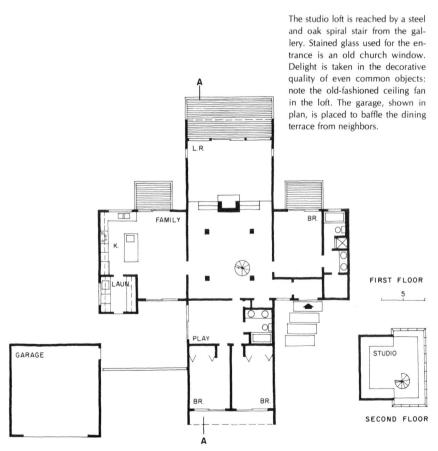

FIRST FLOOR

5

SECOND FLOOR

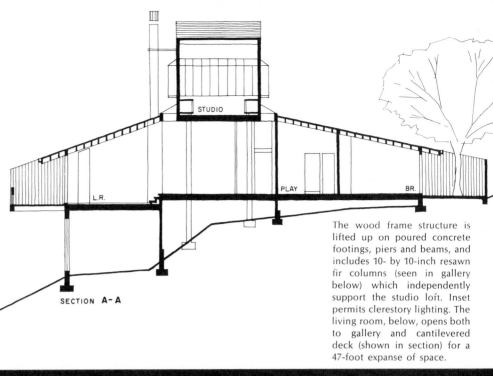

SECTION A-A

The wood frame structure is lifted up on poured concrete footings, piers and beams, and includes 10- by 10-inch resawn fir columns (seen in gallery below) which independently support the studio loft. Inset permits clerestory lighting. The living room, below, opens both to gallery and cantilevered deck (shown in section) for a 47-foot expanse of space.

The owner, a San Francisco graphic artist, required that the house include a work studio set apart from other family rooms. A cross-shaped plan was chosen to provide both space and the privacy the family required. Wings divide the first floor into four zones: living room (below right), kitchen-family room (next page), master bedroom and a special suite for the two daughters, aged seven and nine. Space between wings is put to work for family living as well, as in the outdoor dining space between kitchen and playroom. The central gallery (photos below) is, of course, pivotal, providing quick circulation and letting wings work together in a variety of ways for both general use and special entertaining.

The studio loft which dominates the design, shown in photo above left, forms a fifth, vertical zone off the gallery. Though set apart from the rest of the house as required, this element—which could have been a mere appendage to the living scheme—is instead a natural and very original elaboration of the basic plan.

Architects: Fisher-Friedman Associates. Owners: Mr. and Mrs. Robert Pease. Location: Alamo, California. Engineers: L. F. Robinson & Associates. Contractor: Silver Construction Company.

The house by Fisher-Friedman includes the kitchen-family room which extends onto a rear cantilevered deck (below) and onto the outdoor dining terrace (left). Fifty-year-old oak trees provide shade.

Most floors, with the exception of the quarry-tiled gallery, are laminated, sanded and stained wood. All cabinets are vertical-grained Douglas fir. The island kitchen counter has a chopping block surface. Color comes from red, green and blue rugs, upholstery and enamel cooking ware.

Decks shown in the rear view of the house, above, share a distant view with the horizon some 40 miles off. The tower shed-roof opens to the north to bring work light into the studio. Exterior materials are red cedar shingle roof and 1- by 6-inch resawn redwood siding. All exterior sheet metal is painted black. Dark anodized aluminum sash is used for sliding doors. Materials will weather and age to blend with the woodland.

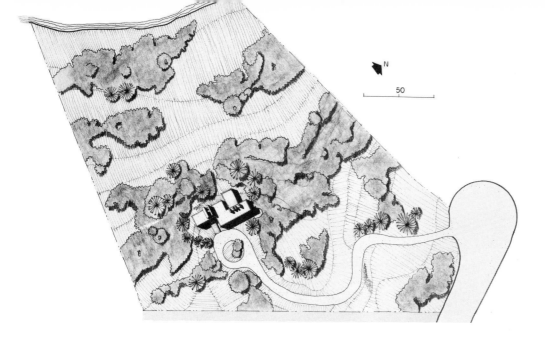

A TRIM AND SOPHISTICATED HOUSE ON A RUGGED LOT

A natural setting of granite outcroppings, hardwood and pine trees makes an unusual counterfoil for the trim, sophisticated house in Dover, Massachusetts by architect Earl Flansburgh, which is shown below and on the following pages. Painted wood siding and concrete block are skillfully used and finely detailed to contrast with the unlandscaped plot.

The house is oriented to exploit a special view of the Charles River and take best advantage of a sloping site, and planned to fulfill typical and special needs of a young suburban family. The many requirements have been handsomely met in an uncluttered scheme in which form, materials and detail are combined in an unfussy, all-of-a-piece design.

Louis Reens photos

Expansiveness, privacy and versatility were among the owners' many requirements. Space for adults' entertaining and children's play had to be provided, as well as space for general family use. A view of the river was an especially important design determinant. The Charles River bounds the site to the east, at the foot of sloping land which the clients own.

By placing the house just below the crest of a knoll which exists at the center of the site, the architect was able to expose the house to the downhill view and shield it from the uphill road. The river determined the orientation of the house and the focus of most rooms. Use was made of the slope to provide a cantilevered deck, a protected terrace and informal living space for jam sessions and dance practice. The plan is Z-shaped to emphasize the orientation while insuring good zoning of living and sleeping areas and good circulation for every room, thus making full use of the site possibilities and fulfilling the clients' requirements.

All architectural elements—materials, spaces, details and finishes—contribute to turn the program solution into the strong architectural statement on which the visual success of the scheme is based. There are two main circulation areas—stair and bedroom corridor—and these were selected for special architectural expression. Ceiling heights jump up at these areas and open out as skylights to create the major spatial interest of the house. Special concrete fins support the skylights, visually anchor the house and create the major design motif.

The house is wood frame using simple span and cantilever construction. Cladding is rough-sawn pine with smooth pine facing. Masonry for the chimney and fins is pumice rock concrete units. Smooth plywood is used for the baffles which shield glass on the exposed side and add a lively, three-dimensional quality to the design. By cantilevering the wood frame slightly from the concrete foundation the architect was able to visually "float" the house over the irregular land and add great strength to the overall design.

Heating is forced warm air with two oil furnaces. The house includes 3,300 square feet.

Architect: Earl R. Flansburgh & Associates—Earl R. Flansburgh and Jane Weinzapfel, design team. *Owners:* Mr. and Mrs. G. Stewart Baird, Jr. *Location:* Dover, Massachusetts. *Engineers:* Souza & True. *Consultants:* Francis Associates. *Contractor:* Sherman J. L. Brown.

126

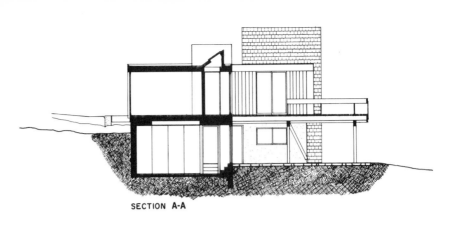

SECTION A-A

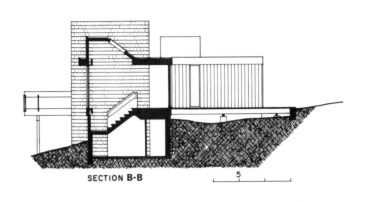

SECTION B-B

5

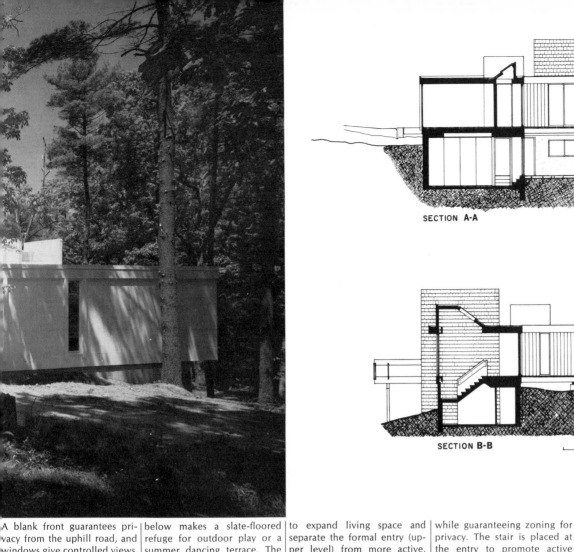

A blank front guarantees privacy from the uphill road, and windows give controlled views. The rear is mostly glass for exposure to the view and for a close relationship with the woods. A "tree house" deck extends living space; the space below makes a slate-floored refuge for outdoor play or a summer dancing terrace. The use of the fin motif, white-painted wood, slightly recessed foundation and constant roof line give overall design unity.

Use of the slope is made to expand living space and separate the formal entry (upper level) from more active, outdoor-indoor traffic (lower level). Skylights are located above main circulation areas and open to the east. The plan permits exposure to the view while guaranteeing zoning for privacy. The stair is placed at the entry to promote active use of the lower level. Generous storage is provided throughout. Children's rooms are placed to ease use of most of the house for adults.

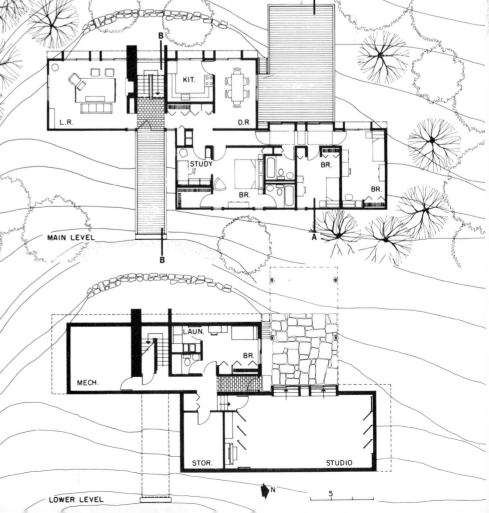

MAIN LEVEL

L.R.   KIT.   D.R.   STUDY   BR.   BR.   BR.

LOWER LEVEL

MECH.   LAUN.   BR.   STOR.   STUDIO

N   5

5: Houses for small lots

Here, typically, we are talking about suburban or urban lots—the kind of site on which America's homebuilders have created so much quantity but not a lot of design quality. But you can have, as the houses in this chapter demonstrate well, many of the advantages inherent in a custom-design house even on this most constricting kind of site.

For many people, and for many different kinds of reasons, the in-town or close-to-town lot is the only solution. Many, of course, prefer to live in the heart of things and want no part of commuting or the quiet of the countryside. For others, job schedules make any more than a few minutes travel from work to home undesirable. But again, as these houses show, with careful design by a good architect you can—on the smallest of lots—create the kind of environment you want, and the setting for the kind of life style you prefer.

What are the design goals you are typically aiming for in a house on this kind of site?

1. Typically, houses on urban or small suburban lots are more formal than houses in the exurbs or the country. Often, country houses—even if they are first houses and lived in year-round—have a vacation-house quality, an informality in plan, in finishes, and even in form that is not appropriate in suburbs or city. The point is obvious—a beach house or a ski house or a mountain cabin simply does not fit in a well-tended suburb.

2. Privacy must be carefully planned. Larger sites create privacy simply by their size; on a small site the privacy must be created by careful placement of rooms and windows and glass doors in those rooms, and sometimes by well-planned fences or walls or screens of shrubbery and trees.

3. Noise privacy, too, must be carefully planned. Not long ago it was simply assumed that the living room ("the parlor") went to the front of the house—now it seldom does. It does not follow, however, that the ideal place for the main living spaces is to the rear; it all depends on the lot shape, on existing plantings, on the lot next door, on the plan of the neighboring houses. In more than a few houses in this chapter you will find the living room opening to the outdoors on the side of the house where a quiet side patio or terrace has been created.

4. Two-story solutions seem almost universal, mostly so that—for a given needed floor area—enough space is left on the lot for outdoor gardens or terraces, and for parking. Which brings up a most interesting point . . .

5. Even on a tight piece of land, provision for the automobile(s) need not be dominant. Drive along most subdivision streets and what do you see? Driveways leading up to garage doors—rows and rows of garage doors. Often the garage doors are painted a different color so that they are the dominant design element on the front of the house. (Many builders, in an effort to change the effect, let the garage door into the side of the house but leave windows on the front façade. This in turn leads to a true abomination: curtains hung in a garage window.)

There are alternative solutions, as the houses in this chapter demonstrate. Despite the fact that they are on small lots, only a few have the garage door facing the street; and in those that do, a major effort has been to balance that utilitarian but unlovely mass with another shape so that the garage door is not "the thing." Indeed, as you study the pictures on these pages, you will have trouble spotting the garage—but it's there (see plan drawings).

6. On these smaller lots, much more attention and much more respect must be paid to the neighbors' houses. This attention goes beyond the mandatory attention to zoning and building codes. It extends to height limits and setback requirements and general character. It takes a bold personality to take a stark white contemporary house into a street of red-brick Colonials. But . . .

This is not to say that you cannot have a thoroughly contemporary house in the midst of the traditional (or fake traditional) houses that line most suburban streets. For every one of the houses in this chapter is thoroughly contemporary.

It does not take small-pane windows and imitation carriage lamps to make a house fit a New England suburban street. A brick or brownstone wall can look perfectly comfortable on a street in New Orleans or New York, and open to a wildly contemporary living space with two-story-high rooms and skylights and great glass walls opening to private courtyards.

7. Unless your idea of a good view is the house across the street (an assumption made by the builders of many subdivisions), on small urban or suburban lots an attempt must be made to create views. This can be done by opening up patios within cut-outs in the house plan. As in traditional houses in warm climates, a central patio is sometimes the solution. Or you can create private

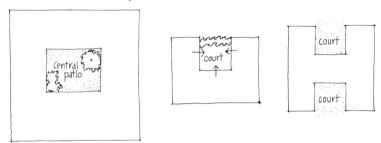

courts opening to one, two, or three different rooms with a U-shaped plan or an H-shaped plan. Under the zoning laws in many cities, you can build up to the lot line, using the house itself as one wall and extending a house-high wall around the site to create spacious but completely private walled yards.

You'll find such houses in this chapter for all kinds of climates, for all kinds of styles of living, for all degrees of preference for "traditional" or contemporary style. These exciting houses demonstrate that—if you prefer to live in the city, or if you must—you have most of the same options that less constraining sites offer; that sensitive design related to your needs and way of living offers the same benefit "close-in" that it does on the most dramatic beach or mountainside.

PRIVACY INDOORS AND OUT
ON A 50-FOOT LOT

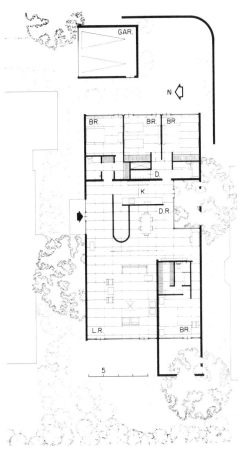

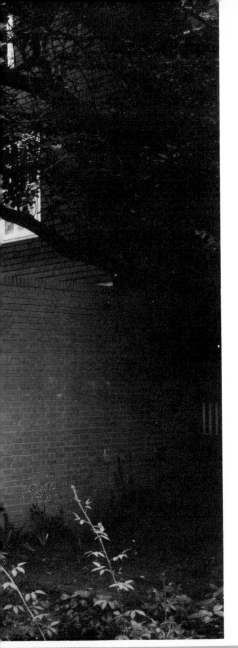

The interiors and the dining table and sofas were designed by the architect. Since the living room is exposed to the outdoors on three sides it is filled with light all day.

Bill Engdahl, Hedrich-Blessing photos

Architect David Haid's home for his family is inserted under the spreading oaks in a neighborhood of large Victorian houses. On a 50- by 150-foot lot, it has both privacy and openness, indoors and out.

The designer, an associate of Mies van der Rohe for several years, sees the house not so much as an expression of the Miesian style as use of a practical design vocabulary to solve a specific residential problem for a specific building lot.

The interior is open in plan except for the children's end which can be closed off. The rest of the house is a 50- by 40-foot space shared quite openly by the living and dining areas and the kitchen, and less so by the master bedroom. A large pantry—the round-ended shape near the middle of the plan—separates the vestibule and dining area. A curtain between the dining and living areas can be drawn during preparations for a dinner party but is more frequently moved around just for fun.

All sections of the house open onto courts which open to the spaces beyond (see plan) so there is a sense of containment rather than confinement. The expansive living room area (30- by 24-feet with the curtain drawn) opens onto a court formed by dense planting which, when fully grown, will make the house almost invisible from the street. This court is open on one side to the front walk. In the court off the kitchen and dining area there is a break in the wall to allow for the presence of a large oak. This break also provides glimpses into nearby yards. As the wall forming a play area outside the children's rooms is overlapped rather than attached, this space flows into the side yard.

The extraordinarily large, column-free, interior spaces were attained by the use of a steel frame roof resting on lead-padded bearing plates on the masonry walls. The glass walls are framed with shop fabricated steel units.

The colors of the structure, black steel fascias and mullions, beige terrazzo floors, gray buff brick walls and white drywall ceilings and partitions —contrast with the exuberant yellow divider curtain and golden orange master bedroom spread, both of Siamese silk.

Architect and owner: David Haid. Location: Evanston, Illinois. Structural engineers: Wiesinger-Holland Ltd. Mechanical and electrical engineers: Wallace and Migdal. Landscape architect: Paul Thomas.

CONTEMPORARY, YET COMFORTABLE ON A CITY STREET

Hugh Stubbins has built a lively, walled-in retreat for himself and his wife, on Cambridge's historic Brattle Street. It stands amongst a long line of Georgian and other-styled houses going back to the house of Henry Wadsworth Longfellow and others of note. Though varied in design, all these houses now carry the general aura of "traditional". On the contemporary change of pace that this house introduces, Stubbins comments: "I wanted my addition to this street to be compatible, but also a reminder of its own era. It is essentially a house for a couple. The idea of the house is one that I have played with in one form or another over the years—it is like a barn with open lofts. In section its guideline geometry is a circle —a satisfying proportion."

The house can, indeed, almost be considered as a single room of very ample and satisfying proportions —with numerous alcoves and spaces that can be closed or left open as desired.

At first glance, the house appears relatively simple in concept, and its corner lot is well screened by an enclosing wall. However, a closer look reveals some of the surprising and intriguing details—all done with discernment and a good dollop of wit. Stubbins explains, "the main room soars 26 feet to the ridge; the structure, raised and dropped girts, ties and the like, are exposed to view. The simple, barn-like form is enlivened by punched holes in the walls for windows, in the roof for skylights; by overhanging the second floor at the ends; by a bay window, a dormer, by opening a whole wall; by hanging a louver for the western sun, and by pergolas and brick walls tying the house into the landscape. The visual secrets and surprises are not immediately revealed."

Architect and owner: Hugh Stubbins.
Location: Cambridge, Massachusetts.
Contractor: H. Tobiason.

Well-designed, well-executed details are a dominant highlight of the Stubbins house. Though some of them are highly individual (note the shuttered "windows" from the upstairs bedrooms into the main room, and the open balcony "hallway"), all also evidence a great love for good materials and finishes. Stubbins comments that the "materials were selected for beauty, simplicity and ease of maintenance. The exterior is rough-sawn redwood, white-painted window trim, asphalt shingles (the building code required fire rating), and waterstruck brick for walls and the terrace around the swimming pool.

"On the interior, the structural Douglas fir is stained dark brown. Dining room and kitchen floors are Welsh tile—the color of old leather; wide oak boards form the floors of the living room, and the entire second floor is carpeted." To highlight these materials, all walls and ceilings are simple rough plaster, painted white, with well-placed accent lights.

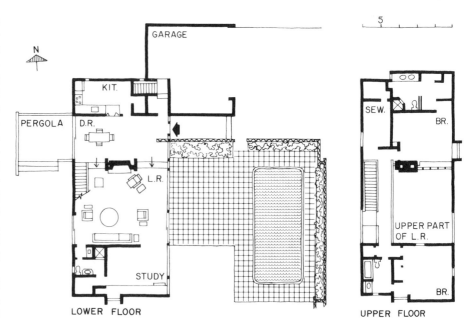

LOWER FLOOR

UPPER FLOOR

Louis Reens, photos

135

John Oldenkamp photos

UPPER LEVEL   N   5

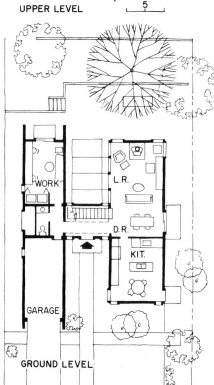

GROUND LEVEL

AN H-SHAPED PLAN CREATES PRIVATE COURTYARDS

Economy and privacy were two important design criteria for architect Paul McKim's own townhouse. Built on a small, narrow lot, flanked on both sides by neighboring houses, the residence affords the McKims a good deal of privacy, and a nice sense of the outdoors.

For a house containing 1,600 square feet of living space, the construction cost was extremely low, especially when the beautifully detailed results are considered. Costs were kept to the budget by using a wood-frame, post-and-beam construction with large plaster panels on both the interior and exterior surfaces.

Basically, the design consists of two rectangular wings linked by a stairwell (see plan at left). The two courtyards, formed between the wings, give the desired outdoor space and privacy.

The house is zoned so that the children use the left wing and the parents the right. This means of zoning seems to be a good answer to maintaining a level of privacy suitable to

both parents and children. The children's bedrooms were placed over the "work" area, which could double as a play room in bad weather.

The interior is enlivened by opening up of the one-story space in the dining area to two-story spaces on both sides—in the living room, and in part of the kitchen.

An especially nice attention to details is evident in this house. Everything—from the trellis which spans the front courtyard and casts strong shadows down the white plaster wall (see photo right), to the hooded balcony over the garage—achieves the greatest effect by the simplest means. Even the white walls of the courtyard serve the secondary purpose of reflecting the sun into the north side of the living room.

Architect and owner: Paul W. McKim. *Location:* San Diego, Calif. *Landscape architect:* Wimmer & Yamada. *Interior designer:* Dixon Morrow Jr. *Contractor:* John Worobec.

Despite such a small budget, he has achieved striking spaces—including the big two-story living room and a variety of outdoor areas as well.

138

Joseph W. Molitor photos

A major factor in the design problems of the house was the big banyan tree shown in the sketch at left (the tree is impossible to photograph—edges of it appear in the two photos here). The plan contains few but good-sized rooms. The child's room is divisible.

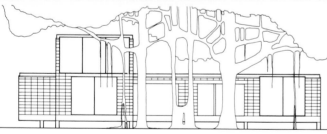

STUDIO

BR.

K.

5

L.R.

BR.

A WHITE SCULPTURE IN A TROPICAL FOREST

"Like a big sculpture perched alone in a rain forest" is architect Singer's comment on this very interesting house he has designed for builder Lewis Weinberger. It is an apt analogy, for the trim concrete and concrete block forms do stand in sharp and sympathetic contrast to the site—part of a tract previously used as a nursery and now overgrown with such lush tropical vegetation as an 80-foot spreading banyan tree. Singer adds: "The shelter of that tree was desirable, but its root structure is devastating to anything resting on or within three feet of the surface of the earth."

"The solution to this was a foundation system designed as a series of short columns penetrating the root system and bearing on concrete pads poured below the problem level. Thus the masonry house floats serenely three feet off the ground."

The house is also well-geared to its tropical setting in other ways: tall rooms, cool and easy-to-keep surfaces, and an electric heat pump for year-round air conditioning.

In all floor, wall and roof systems used in the house, the structural material also provides the finish. Concrete beams span the distance between the foundation posts and carry precast floor joists which were set in the formwork of the beams; the flooring itself is of 2-foot-square reinforced-cement tiles.

All walls are concrete block, reinforced with concrete and steel. Precast concrete lintels span over openings to support the loads of the 4-inch laminated wood decking, which forms both roof and finished ceiling. Ductwork for the heating and air conditioning is carried to all areas of the house in a plenum over the hallway.

Architect: Donald Singer. *Owners:* Mr. and Mrs. Lewis Weinberger. *Location:* Miami, Florida. *Engineers:* Houha & Harry Associates. *Contractor:* Lewis Weinberger.

The living room (above and left) rises to a two-story height, and has a big clerestory window over the skylighted dining area. A little deck separates master bedroom (below) from the child's room.

James O. Milmoe

AN URBANE HOUSE FOR AN URBAN LOT

Creating space and privacy for a restricted city site is a pressing problem graciously met in this trim and elegant home for a family of five. The very personal environment is quite removed from the busy city scene, but imparts a quality of sophisticated precision that reflects urban character at its best. Since the owners already owned a ski house in the Colorado mountains, it was their wish that the Denver townhouse be, in contrast, suited to a formal city style, and at the same time adapted to the varied entertainment requirements of an active social and civic life. The small, flat city lot, removed from the street, suggested the house's compact, two-story scheme. Community and privacy are both assured by basic zoning of the plan—adult activities to the front, with formal areas below and private above, and children's areas and utilities to the rear. All are connected along an organizing central axis, and pivot on a central skylighted spiral stair. Dining and living rooms, gallery and library knit into this axis and can be closed off as formal rooms or fused together for open-house use. A skylighted entrance gallery helps to articulate the upstairs plan while providing a focal point for rooms below. Special elements—including a guest suite and basement sauna—are also neatly incorporated.

Architect: Carl Groos, Jr.—Mardi B. Groos, associate. *Owners:* Mr. and Mrs. William V. Warren, Jr. *Location:* Denver, Colorado. *Structural engineer:* B. W. Lorance. *Mechanical engineer:* John Blank.

Axial views with their framed vistas are used as a design motif throughout and provide a sense of depth to the compact volume of the house. This spatial design, a classical device illustrated in the photos of gallery, dining and living rooms below, reveals the rich contrasts that make walking—as well as looking—through the house a pleasurable experience, and at the same time reflects the orderly and practical arrangement of its functions.

Marc Neuhof photos

Facades of the Warren house reflect the owners' request for open, but restrained formality. Glazed areas on three sides are ample, but never aggressive, and are subordinated to the symmetrical scheme. Warm beige brick, imported from Mexico, contrasts with the crisp lines of dark wood sash. The same carefully integrated precision of parts and good materials is carried throughout the interior. Brick and highly polished granite are used in the cool, formal gallery (photo below), and contrast with the rich wood parquet floors of the living areas beyond. Polished beige flagstone over concrete is used for kitchen and baths. The owners collect fine antiques, and both these more ornate pieces and the simpler contemporary furniture are complemented by the timeless quality of both materials and design. The entrance gallery shown below, with its bridge linking upstairs master suite and children's quarters, combines spatial formality and inventiveness in a counterpoint that keynotes the house's design.

SECOND FLOOR

FIRST FLOOR   5

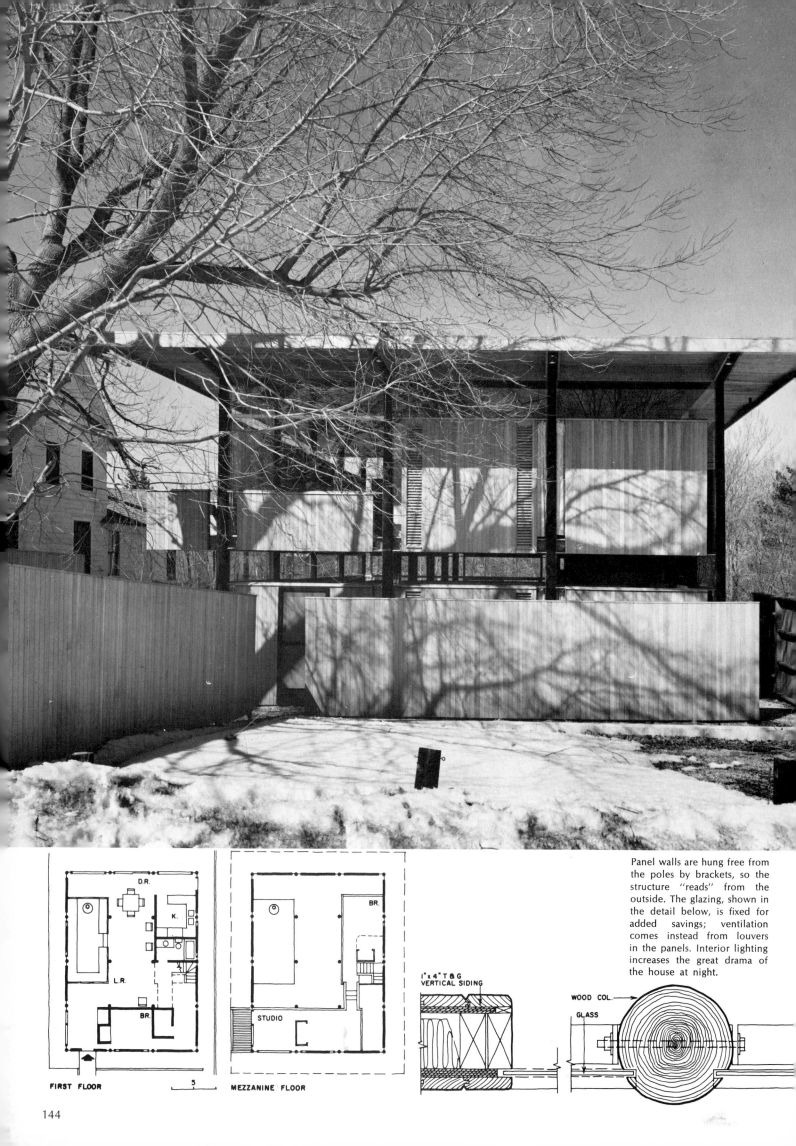

Panel walls are hung free from the poles by brackets, so the structure "reads" from the outside. The glazing, shown in the detail below, is fixed for added savings; ventilation comes instead from louvers in the panels. Interior lighting increases the great drama of the house at night.

FIRST FLOOR

D.R.

K.

L.R.

BR.

MEZZANINE FLOOR

BR.

STUDIO

5

1"x4" T&G
VERTICAL SIDING

WOOD COL.

GLASS

A SOPHISTICATED POLE HOUSE FOR THE SUBURBS

Economy and a great sense of space have been achieved for this sophisticated little weekend house by its ingenious structure composed of a system of 20-foot-high wood poles.

The house was designed for a single client who came to the architect with a small budget and a 60-foot-wide suburban lot. This had houses on three sides and no interesting site features except one large tree. The architect's idea was to make up in the interior space what was lacking in the site: the interior volume was to be a site itself.

A seven-foot-high fence and wooden curtain walls were strategically placed to block off neighbors, and visually preserve a sense of airiness and light. The poles support the space, but do not break it up.

Placed on a grid of room-sized 10-foot bays, these poles carry roof, balcony and panel loads, and create a marvelously expansive flow of space which admirably fulfills the architect's intent—but keeps within the client's budget.

Privacy is assured inside, and space usage defined, by changes in level which add to the drama of the structural frame. A living "room" is two steps down; the owner's bedroom, guest room and study are tucked in mezzanines bolted to the poles. "The different elevations," comments the architect, give "controlled views of the foliage and sky—up and out" as well as secluded lookouts on the inside space below.

The design strength of the little house derives as much from the expression of these natural wood materials, which are left exposed, as from the dynamic organization of the single space and the strong, contrasting geometry of the structural frame.

Architect: Richard Owen Abbott. *Owner:* Miss Joan Traverso. *Location:* Westbrook, Connecticut. *Interior design:* Richard O. Abbott. *Contractor:* George C. Field Co.

A study-balcony, right, shelters the entry and extends through the outside wall as a deck for added open space. The sunken sitting area focuses on the red-painted stove-pipe chimney. Sparing use of primary colors adds spatial depth throughout.

Norman McGrath photos

A SPACIOUS
CALIFORNIA HOUSE
ON A SMALL LOT

Richard Gross photos

A post-and-beam structure in the California-modern tradition is used skillfully in this spacious house for a small suburban lot in the Santa Monica mountains. The major living areas are oriented with decks and pool to overlook a fine view. Here, as throughout, architecture, landscape and site combine to offer informal living with a dramatic flair for an active four-member family. The great variety of indoor and outdoor relationships and outlooks has been both created and controlled by skillful structural technique, whose surprising simplicity can be noted above. But the major architectural challenge—all-too-common a problem, and here, uncommonly well met—was to complete the sizeable house within a medium budget—and complete it without skimping on good materials and good craftsmanship essential to this kind of strong, exposed-structure design.

Architects: Dorman/Munselle. *Owners:* Mr. and Mrs. Harry Mullikin. *Location:* West Los Angeles, California. *Engineer:* Joe Kinoshita. *Landscape architects:* Dorman/Munselle. *Contractor:* Donald Buhler.

The outdoors pervades this house, but there is also a great sense of shelter. Living and kitchen areas borrow space from each other and from the outside, and are easily accessible but clearly separated in an open plan. The family room, in foreground of the photo above, has a pass-through counter into a spacious but compact island kitchen. This, as shown in the large photo, opens as well onto the glass-enclosed breakfast alcove, shown also in the photo from the garden, right.

Redwood beams, exposed redwood tongue-and-grooved sheathing, plaster, and slab floors compose the materials of the house. Walks are beach-stone aggregate. Cabinets are walnut. Heating is forced air.

The house is well placed on a difficult "flag-shape" lot, and shares a motor court with another house close by. Thus the entrance side is screened off and somewhat formal, with large glass areas reserved for southern exposure and outlook to the rear. Small gardens are created behind stucco baffle walls in the front.

A basic "H"-shaped scheme zones bedrooms from activity areas, provides an entry easily accessible to both, and admits light and air throughout. This simple three-part plan suits the structure well, and is effectively framed by it. Exposed beams are handsomely finished, logically placed on a seven-foot module, and always expressive of spatial organization—often dramatically so. Note especially the walkway and entry. In living areas, open planning reinforces glass walls for an over-all flow of space. Freestanding elements—white-brick fireplace and walnut cabinets—interplay with the strongly exposed redwood structural members while effectively zoning functions.

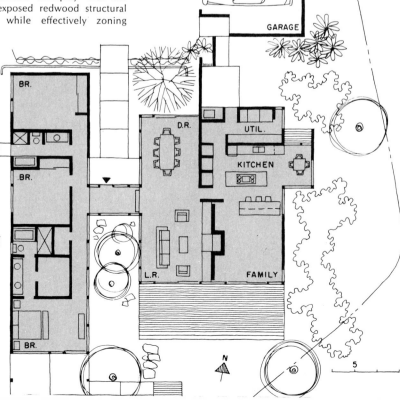

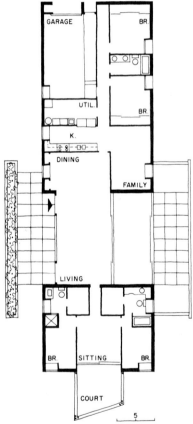

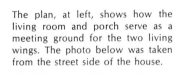

The plan, at left, shows how the living room and porch serve as a meeting ground for the two living wings. The photo below was taken from the street side of the house.

AN INWARD-TURNING HOUSE FOR A FLORIDA LOT

"The basic construction of this house is as simple as it could be made; bearing block walls, flat roof, and stock casement windows all make it pretty standard." Architect Seibert further states that his reason for keeping construction simple was to give the client architecture for a "builder price".

With only a narrow, 50-foot-wide lot to work with, Mr. Seibert used the heavily-planted neighboring lots for the view from the living room and porch, but the remainder of the spacious four-bedroom house turns inward, one wing to the walled court off the sitting room. All windows, except the large ones in the living room, are shielded from the sun by louvered shutters, giving the house a regional flavor and a sense of self-containment.

Architect: Edward J. Seibert. *Owners:* Mr. and Mrs. Cooney. *Location:* Sarasota, Florida. *Interior designer:* Terry L. Rowe & Associates. *Contractor:* Thyne Construction Company.

Wade Swicord photos

On the exterior, the stucco applied over concrete block adds to the regional quality of the house. The sphere seen in the photos at left is a lamp. Many more plantings are planned to shield the house from its neighbors.

Ceilings and interior walls are drywall, while the roof is wood-framed, built-up.

The comfortably furnished interior is fully air-conditioned. The walled court shows in the photo, right.

AN ATRIUM HOUSE—PRIVACY ON A CROWDED STREET

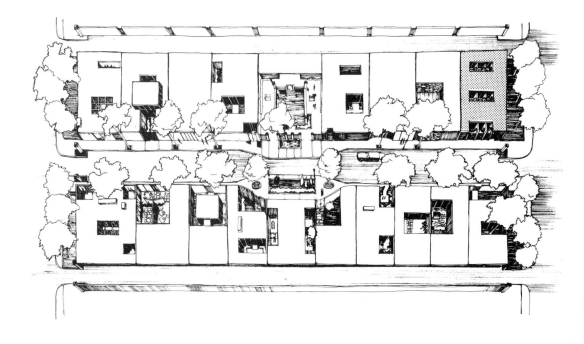

The traditional "townhouse" concept has been successfully revived in this southern house, one of a group of custom-designed row houses for a Houston development planned by the architect. Stylistically, the houses are all quite contemporary, but the use of similar and fairly traditional materials gives a unified, almost "timeless" quality.

The development is built in the midst of a typical city subdivision which has large lawns and traditional houses built out to 10 foot restriction lines at the sides of each lot. By planning this new development as a unit, it was possible to extend the encompassing walls of each house to the lot lines. A communal swimming pool and recreation pavilion are placed at the center of the development. Service alleys range the back of each block of houses.

This house is built on a corner lot of the area, on a site measuring 45 by 75 feet. To minimize the space required, a carport was devised for parking sideways at the back, off the service alley. Vistas are provided for each room inside the house by a series of patios formed by colonnades of brick arches. The arches carry through the house as a design motif.

Architect and owner: Preston M. Bolton. *Location:* Houston, Texas. *Structural Engineer:* R. George Cunningham. *Contractor:* Stewart & Stewart Construction Company.

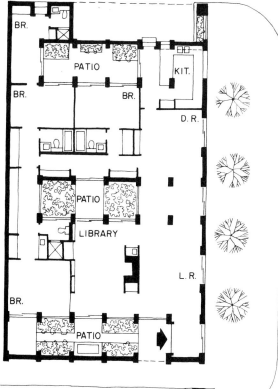

Behind the 12-foot-high paneled doors at the entrance of the Bolton house lies a series of rooms with a startling sense of spaciousness—a quality which is unfortunately not adequately conveyed by the photographs. The owners state that: "People are continually amazed that we have four bedrooms and four baths, each with its own patio view in this limited space, but the living area of our house has been considerably increased by the garden courts. We have small bedrooms and this is the way we like to live—with a minimum of furniture and maximum use of organized dress- ing room storage. Our favorite place is the library with its walls of books and glass: one way we look out on a patio with a fountain of playing water; the other way, to a tropical garden with swaying palms. We like our house and wouldn't change a thing."

The interior organization of the house is also a very conveniently and flexibly arranged one. For example, the library is placed where it may be used with the living area for entertaining, or with the master bedroom to form a private apartment. The library and living room are divided by a fireplace enclosed in natural

finish walnut with white divider strips.

The kitchen is placed for direct service in the living-dining area or the rear patio, and adjoins the carport to ease the handling of groceries and deliveries. The maid's quarters at the back also have an entrance through the rear patio, which doubles in function as a children's play area. The child's bedroom, bath and dressing room open both from the maid's room and the master bedroom corridor to afford surveillance. The fourth bedroom, bath and dressing room, forms a guest suite. Along the side of the house flanking the public street, are a series of arched windows, shielded by walnut shutters to allow complete privacy or openness, as one desires.

The structure of the house is wood

Edward A. Bourdon photos

frame on a concrete slab, with exterior walls of champagne-colored Mexican brick and concrete block. Interior walls are white-painted wall board, brick and walnut paneling; floors are dark oak with borders of white tile.

6: Houses for sloping sites

Many people, including many experienced homebuilders, think of sloping sites as problem sites. They do indeed require some special attention, especially in foundations and in the handling of the water that, inevitably, comes rolling down the hill to the house.

But most architects look upon sloping sites as opportunities—opportunities to design houses with exciting views and exciting spaces within. And the houses in this chapter (as well as the steep-site houses in the following chapter) are the proof of that pudding—they include some of the most dramatic and livable houses in the entire collection.

In the hands of a good architect, the design of any house begins with the slope of that hill. As you study the houses on the next pages, you will find that every one of them, in various ways, relates to that slope and, most importantly, minimizes the disturbance of the hill.

poles

The house on the next page is a pole house—poles are driven into the ground until they hit rock or enough resistance to support the load of the house, and all of the floor beams and roof rafters are bolted to and supported by the poles. This system probably disturbs a site the least.

pad
grade beam

Two other houses rest on concrete piers which in turn are supported by concrete pads or grade beams.

In these houses, there is little or no cutting of the hill or earthmoving. And this structural solution minimizes the problem of handling drainage—water rolling down the hill simply continues on its way unhindered.

cut   fill

There are, of course, advantages to notching the hill—primarily the creation of extra and relatively low-cost basement space. But, you will notice, in the section-through-the-house drawings on the pages that follow, that the degree of notching or cutting away of the hill is quite modest.

too big a cut

heavy water pressure

Notching the hill too deeply creates several complications, the prime one being water pressure on the wall. A room-high wall notched into a hillside needs to be very strong, and perhaps buttressed against water pressure; and unless oversize drains are set to lead the water away from the wall, which needs to be well waterproofed in any case, leaking is almost inevitable. As many homebuyers know to their sorrow, conventional basements are prone enough to leak. On hillsides, the pressure is greater because the water is in motion down the hill.

How do you avoid a too-deep notch? One way is to look for natural cuts into which the house can be fitted, as in the drawing.

Another solution that can be used to advantage is a small cut-and-fill, as shown in the drawing. In this system, the dirt and rock from a shallow notch is used to fill behind a low wall, creating a pad for the house to rest on.

And another solution is the split-level. This design device, so often abused, makes perfect sense for sloping sites (see drawing). With attention to floor levels, rooms on both the up- and downhill sides of the house can be opened to grade.

At any rate, there are endless solutions and combinations of solutions to fitting a house into the site. Above that foundation solution, there are few design constraints as—again—you will see as you study the houses in this chapter.

There do seem to be some general rules:

Most hillside houses are a bit freer, a bit more informal than the average house. Natural materials seem appropriate—like rough board finishes, exposed beams, stone from the site. Most hillside houses make effective use of decks, since it is often cheaper and more appropriate to open a room to a cantilevered or post-supported deck than it is to arrange rooms and/or slope so that rooms can open to on-grade terraces.

There are all kinds of opportunities for exciting spaces in hillside houses. Typically, floor levels change—as in a split-level arrangement—and under a conventional roof plane this creates rooms of different heights. In many of the houses you will see in this chapter and the following one on steep sites, three levels of rooms are possible, sometimes with rooms opening from balconies to tall adjacent spaces.

The development of stairways is important to create logical and comfortable progressions from one space to another. More than a few hillside houses have circular staircases. They are dramatic and handsome, and use a minimum of space, but for many people they are not comfortable. And families with young children and/or elderly members should approach this design solution with caution.

The main rooms of a hillside house—the living and dining rooms—typically are placed to look down the hill to the best view. Sometimes, these main spaces are properly placed on the highest level, where they can gain a view over the treetops to the view beyond.

157

Morley Baer photos

A south slope, densely wooded with Monterey Pines and overlooking Carmel Bay, is the site for this handsome pole house designed for sale by architects Smith & Larson. The decision to use pole supports simplified the foundation conditions, left the site as undisturbed as possible and, in general, minimized the difficulties and expense conventionally associated with building on a hillside.

Living spaces are arranged on three levels. Kitchen, dining, living room and master bedroom share the lowest level. Carport, study, guest room and bath occupy the middle level. The upper level is reserved for children's lofts and storage. Entrance and lofts face the street while the living areas open toward the south and the view.

The poles form an exterior framing system standing just outside the plane of the walls except that the lower level living spaces pivot around a single freestanding pole that supports a corner of the study above.

The house was built as a speculative venture by architects who wanted to expand their experience as they established their practice. In the absence of an owner with a precise program, the house might have become too personal—too fervid an expression of the designers' own attitudes and interests. Happily, that did not happen. While the conception is anything but timid, the apportionment of spaces is clearly functional and the designers have carefully avoided geometric extremes or oddly shaped volumes.

As a result, the house found an enthusiastic buyer almost at once. Lawrence Spector speaks lyrically of his new house: "I wanted to own it after we opened the front door . . . light, space, view in every direction . . . rain water running down the sheets of roof glass. We were under a waterfall. I could have indoor plants, a natural kind of decoration everywhere.

"I walked around the property in the next days, in the light of day, in the rain, at midnight. The house simply radiates from any position on the land. . . ."

This praise is not undeserved. The Spector house is beautifully tailored to its site and apparently just as well suited to the needs of its new owner.

Architects and engineers: Smith & Larson. *Owner:* Lawrence Albert Spector. *Location:* Pebble Beach, California. *General Contractor:* Smith & Larson.

A HOUSE PERCHED ABOVE THE SITE ON POLES

The main entrance (photo left) is reached by means of a stair and bridge at the side of the house. The bridge is protected from the weather by the projection of the level above. A simply detailed deck (photo right) extends beyond the living room and provides an intimate space for outdoor dining.

Sunlight is brought deep into the interior of the living-dining space by glass panels cut into the pitched roof (photos right and above left). The second floor study draws sunlight from the same source. Thanks to careful design, the quality of natural light is exceptionally pleasant throughout the house.

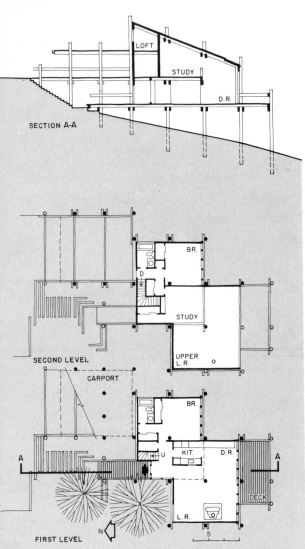

SECTION A-A

LOFT
STUDY
D.R.

SECOND LEVEL

CARPORT

BR.

STUDY

UPPER
L.R.

BR.

KIT.   D.R.

DECK

L.R.

A   A

N

FIRST LEVEL

5

Morley Baer photos

From the entry, circulation steps both down the slope to the living areas, and up, with the daughter's bedroom branching off along the way. Master bedroom is at the top.

LOWER LEVEL   5

UPPER LEVEL

A TALL NARROW HOUSE ON A HILL

All kinds of varied and festive spaces—big and small, secluded and open—have been packed into this little redwood-clad house. Because the lot was very small, the house goes up instead of out, and makes use of its height for the added impact of changing outlooks over a canyon of eucalyptus trees and oaks, and the Bay of Monterey beyond. Many kinds of windows – including a big picture window in the master bedroom tower, a slit window, and sliding doors to the deck – exploit these long-range vistas and close-up views of plants and branches. Other visual surprises, from a balcony and a bridge across the stair, concentrate on the indoor spaces of the house, and seem to expand its actual size.

The site, favored with privacy to the south, is described by the architect as "a triangular handkerchief of hillside, encumbered for most of its area by set-backs. . . . The general environs contain residual agricultural uses and encroaching subdivision housing; the access road being a disorganized collision of the two." This situation ordained that the approach side be relatively closed, with the result that entry is an added discovery and surprise.

The owners—a professor and his artist wife—wanted a bright, cheery, sunny house, and everything has been done to obtain it. Walls are painted white to push them out. Colors come from paintings and the many objects that populate the rooms. "A mirrored wall at the entry," continues the architect, "captures and doubles the space of the house and playfully relocates the sun throughout."

For all its "playful illusion," the house is planned with a realistic eye. Carefree materials include redwood siding and a cedar-shingle roof; exposed fir decking; white-painted gypsum board and oak flooring inside.

Architect: MLTW/Moore Turnbull (William Turnbull Jr.; Charles W. Moore). *Owners:* Mr. and Mrs. Dennis McElrath. *Location:* Santa Cruz, California. *Engineers:* Davis & Morreau. *Contractor:* Charles Davis

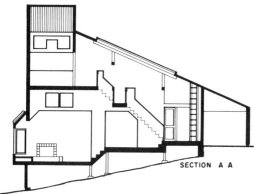

SECTION A A

The great strength of this little house derives from its firm anchorage to the hillside, and from the dominance of its shed-roofed tower. The view to the right shows the central, skylit, two-story hall, from which the view of the living room, below, was taken.

CLASSIC SIMPLICITY
IN CONTEMPORARY FORM

In this house, basically simple, are qualities far from simple to attain which give it a distinction beyond the aspiration of most small houses. It has a plainness like that of Shaker houses, and a clarity, timeless but characteristic of the work of its architect, Joseph Esherick. Set on a steep hillside which had been badly guarded by a previous owner, the house is T-shaped, with the cross bar containing all the rooms but the studio (which also acts as a third bedroom). The quality of light in the houses he designs is important to Joe Esherick: he speaks of designing light, not windows, and here he has provided the principal spaces with unusual and beautiful light, changing through the day and through the seasons, since light is reflected from the hill behind the house, its color influenced by the color of the grass, green in spring, later buckskin.

Architects: Esherick Homsey Dodge and Davis. *Owners:* Mr. and Mrs. Daniel Romano. *Location:* Kentfield, California. *Contractor:* Skaggs Construction Company.

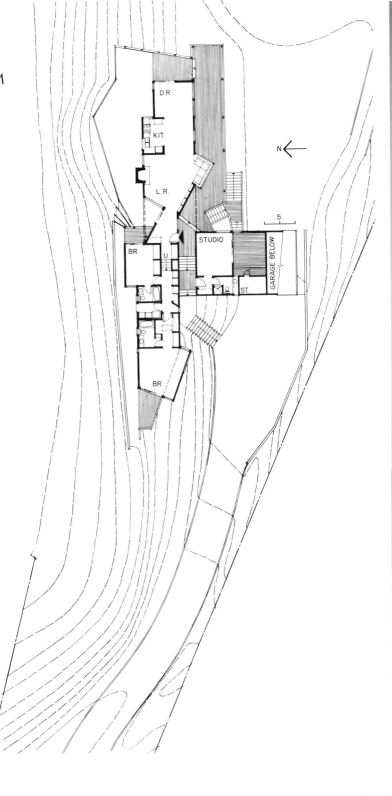

Robert Brandeis photos

Steve Rosenthal photos

TREE-HOUSE, FAMILY SIZE

Truro is a small community located near the northern tip of Cape Cod. The peninsula narrows abruptly near Truro to a minimum width of half a mile, granting many residents views of both the ocean and the bay. The land is tufted with scrub pine and pocked by small glacial basins.

This summer house for a minister and his family, designed by architect Paul Krueger, stands at the lip of one such basin and steps down into its depth to provide a measure of privacy for the lower level bedroom. A twelve-foot-wide, three-level volume, the house is framed in tripled 2 by 12s diagonally braced at top and bottom. Additional bracing—against high winds—is provided by external guy wires turnbuckled to "dead men" at either side of the house (see

photo above).

Built on an extraordinarily modest construction budget, the house is clad in cedar board and batten, exposed on the exterior, and joined to the main vertical structure by horizontal nailers. Floors are fir decking and the roof is finished in cedar shingle. Minimum enclosure, simple construction, minor requirements for equipment, and the sparing use of interior finishes kept costs at rock bottom. But in spite of these economies, the Mark house has a freshness and inventiveness that derives from its siting and the playfulness of its forms. The interior spaces open outward and upward to expand the 12-foot-width and provide easy avenues of visual release. Inside and out, the house has a consistent vocabulary of de-

tails and a pleasant sense of leisure and relaxed informality. It is a house where wet bathing suits do not seem out of place.

Future plans include a small bedroom wing to be constructed farther down the slope and attached to the main structure by a stepped bridge. When the addition is complete, the existing lower level bedroom will become a family room.

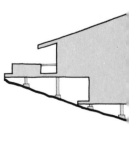

Architect: Paul H. Krueger. *Associate architect:* Malcolm Montague Davis. *Owner:* Reverend and Mrs. Edward L. Mark. *Location:* Truro, Massachusetts. *Structural engineers:* Tsaing Engineering; *structural consultant:* Souza and True. *Contractor:* Colp Brothers.

The approach to the house is a 12-foot-wide bridge-deck that provides a pleasant, sequestered setting for outdoor dining. It also introduces a design theme that will be expanded when the planned bedroom wing is added farther down the basin.

The architect had hoped to expose the braced, structure over the roof but was barred from doing so by local code.

UPPER LEVEL

STUDY

DECK

ENTRY LEVEL

K   D.R   L.R.

5

LOWER LEVEL

BR.   DECK

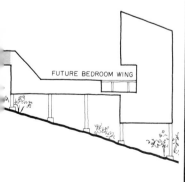

FUTURE BEDROOM WING

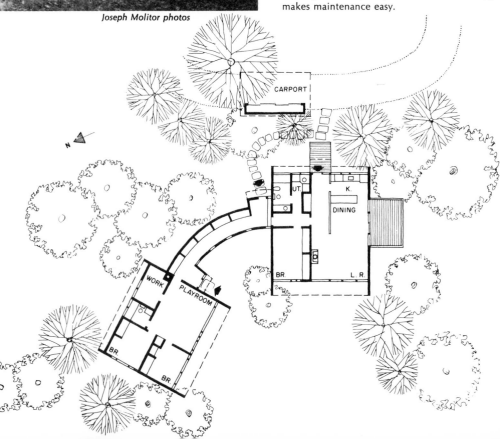

A TWO-ZONE HOUSE THAT FOLLOWS THE SLOPE

Joseph Molitor photos

The Hunters have placed each wing on one of the two natural levels of the land. The connecting helix exactly follows the slope between the wings, as can be seen in the photograph on the left. For rental purposes the children's work area could convert to a kitchen. To get extra space in the summer the outside deck doubles as a dining area. A simple wood frame is articulated by exposing the interior posts and beams. Continuity between the interior and exterior is achieved by carrying the beams out to the overhang and minimizing the window framing. The simplicity and cleanness of design makes maintenance easy.

In designing this house with separate facilities for parents and children, E. H. and M. K. Hunter have also solved the problem of what to do with a large house after the children have gone away to school. Two separate wings linked by a helix-shaped hallway give the parents and children privacy. Eventually, the hallway can be closed off, creating two complete houses. Since only blank walls of the two wings face each other, privacy would be maintained.

Stone for the exposed foundation, pried from rocky ledges on the site, and rough-sawn redwood siding blend with the surrounding New Hampshire woods. Simplicity, an inherent characteristic of this house, is especially evident in the sensitively detailed and proportioned windows. The roof overhang and wall extensions sharply define the windows and shield the interior from sun.

Interior details are handled with the same meticulous care as the exterior. The open plan of each wing appears large for a relatively small area. A prefabricated fireplace and chimney helped to save on construction costs, which were a major consideration. Although the house is quite modern, the clients' own tastes in furnishings seem to fit well. Yellow cabinets on an orange wall were used to brighten up the kitchen area.

Architects: E. H. and M. K. Hunter. *Owners:* Mr. and Mrs. Desmond Canavan. *Location:* Hanover, New Hampshire.

FANCIFUL SHAPES AND FINE FINISHES IN OREGON

Anchored on a ridge among stands of tall trees, this house for a Portland family makes a virtue of ordered irregularity and takes fine advantage of some of the most splendid views to be found anywhere in the Northwest.

All exterior photos: Larry Hudetz

All interior photos: Ron Green

Starting with a steeply contoured site southwest of Portland—a site that offers arresting views to the north and northwest—architects Martin and Soderstrom planned a complex, three-level house for a couple with two teenage daughters. Dominated by a massive masonry core, the house is organized so that support spaces are located in the core or on the blind side while prime spaces open generously to the view of valley floor and mountains beyond. The necessary degree of intra-family privacy is achieved by sensible vertical and horizontal zoning (see floor plans and transverse section on facing page).

What is perhaps most appealing about the house is the way that consistent detailing and use of materials have united an almost unmanageable assortment of projections, intersections, roof slopes and window openings. Visual rhythms are all but absent. But this complexity of plan and massing is clearly not the result of vagrant afterthought. It is an integral part of the planning and contributes a spirit of relaxed informality. This is a house that depends for much of its success on energetic but unifying detail and really superior craftsmanship. Happily, it got both.

Architects: Martin & Soderstrom. Location: Portland, Oregon. Structural engineers: Werner Storch & Associates, Inc.: General contractor: Architectural Construction Company. Interiors: Robert Weller Design in collaboration with Martin & Soderstrom.

The plans contain several unexpected or personal elements. Over the entrance stair, a small playroom anticipates the arrival of grandchildren. It is reached only by an accommodation ladder from the stair itself. On the lower level, light is introduced into the back of the family room by an unusual device—an inside window into a daughter's bedroom. A loom room, part of the upstairs master bedroom suite, is used by the owner's wife. Finally, extending out from under the detached garage, the owner has a workshop turned out toward the timbered valley. The use of sapwood in the cedar siding, both inside and out, lends lively visual interest. Further interest is achieved by decks that extend living and dining spaces toward the view.

SECTION A-A

UPPER FLOOR

BR.

L.R. BELOW

LOOM

ST.

GARAGE

DECK

D.R.

L.R.

A

A

K

UT.

MAIN FLOOR

BR.

FAMILY

BAR

BR.

LOWER FLOOR

The interiors are designed and executed with the same respect for material and attention to detail. Cedar siding is carried inside for continuity where it contrasts in color and texture with gypsum board and concrete block. Windows are double glazed and trimmed with fir. The over-all result is a series of spaces that are comfortable, view oriented, and—even on a gray, winter day—invested with visual warmth.

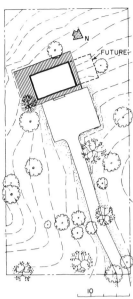

By strategic placement of three skylights in this house in the woods, architect Hugh Jacobsen has created—within a simple and disciplined exterior—an interior space in which the play of light flows naturally from vibrant to soporific. Two of the skylights are in the kitchen area where their light reflects off the wall, over and around the free-standing cabinets, into the living room. The other skylight, which can be seen in the photo below, caps a cylindrical staircase and lets light enter both levels of the house from above.

Additional visual excitement is evoked by the interplay of two primary forms—the cylinder and the rectangle—which stand as dramatic foils to the looser forms of the surrounding trees. Yet the vertical red-cypress siding identifies well with the site and adds a feeling of warmth to the exterior.

Photos by Robert C. Lautman

The architect used the natural slope to its best advantage by providing direct access to both levels. Inside, the two-story cylinder housing the pre-fabricated steel spiral stair is surfaced in white oak flooring, and forms a strong focal point on both levels. The small room behind the kitchen (see plan) contains the mechanical equipment and is entered from the outside.

Under a program calling for a room for each of the Gainer's two children, a master bedroom and playroom, along with living room, dining room and kitchen, the architect produced a plan that allows the house to grow as does the family. Eventually, a master bedroom will be added on to the living room level (to the right of the entrance) along with a master bath. Then by removing the duct- and conduit-free partition, which now separates the playroom and the master bedroom, a much larger playroom will be obtained. An illusion of spaces greater than the actual dimensions of the house is achieved by using floor-to-ceiling glass, the open plan and overhead down-lighting.

On the exterior, the siding of 1- by 4-inch tongue and groove, butt-joint red cypress, is separated from the roof fascia by a 1-inch black slot. The fascia itself, in the same plane as the siding, is, in the architect's words, "the design's deliberate attempt to express a taut skin holding rather large spaces within". The roof is 5-ply built-up, and all sash is anodized black aluminum, sliding glass doors. The deck and rail (see above) are cypress, supported by black-painted, 1-inch-square steel posts. These posts and the mounted down-lights, whose shape echoes the stairwell cylinder, are the only surfaces requiring paint on the outside—the cypress siding was treated only with a clear wood-sealer to preserve its natural color.

Architect: Hugh Newell Jacobsen. *Owner:* Gainer. *Location:* Arlington, Virginia. *Mechanical engineer:* Carl Hansen. *Contractor:* John Clayborne.

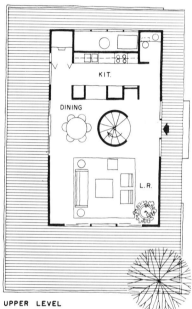

UPPER LEVEL

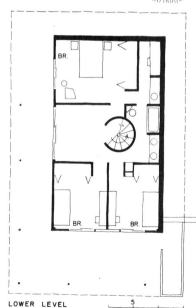

LOWER LEVEL 5

7. Houses for steep sites

A steep site is a very special kind of site; and it asks for a very special kind of house. This is no place for the timid, for lovers of the conventional or the formal, for the lawn-and-garden lover. You just can't have what most people think of as a traditional house on a steep hillside. It's almost bound to require a lot of ramps or steps, so a steep-site house is no place for the elderly (or even the none-too-nimble of any age). The site itself is bound to have places to fall from, so it's no place for little children.

But if you are the right kind of family, the rewards of living on a steep site can be fantastic. Typically, the steep site has a grand view—either a tree-house setting opening to views across the valley, or downwards to a rushing stream or a lake or river, or (as in the Hollywood hills) a brightly lighted city. Think of the number of times, out for a drive, you've stopped to admire the view from a scenic height; and then think about how nice it would be to live there. And you can—in a special kind of house that copes with the problems of such a site and takes full advantage of its opportunities.

And houses on steep sites can offer all kinds of exciting spaces—tall rooms, cantilevered decks for outdoor living, rooftop sun-bathing platforms, soaring bridges leading to the front door.

As in the houses in the preceding chapter, the first and major problem is creating a stable pad on which to put the house. As on a sloping site, you can use poles or pilings—as slender as the trees on the site—and build the house on this base just like a tree house.

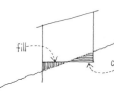

Or, even on a steep site, you can cut and fill at least a modest pad for the foundation of the house.

Another especially dramatic solution, used in the house on the next four pages, is to establish a series of small level spaces, perhaps just room size, cascading down the mountainside and connected by an internal stairwell leading from top to bottom. This house demonstrates rather spectacularly and in a very special way the general rule that it is important to minimize any disruption—any cutting and filling—of the site. This house is quite a large house, but by making the space up from a lot of small spaces, no excessive earthmoving or disruption of the site was required.

But this "minimum disruption" principle can be met in a number of more conventional ways.

One is to simply make the house vertical—to gain the necessary room space by going up (to three or perhaps even four stories) instead of going out as you might on a flat site. The house at Sea Ranch (page 190) explains this idea clearly: it is a three-story tower, hexagonal in shape, with a living-dining room and kitchen on the main level, bedroom and bath above, and an open sleeping/living roof deck above that (space that could have been enclosed if more bedroom space had been needed). And, while this house was built on piers, the section drawing of the house shows clearly that with only minor notching of the slope, a fourth level could have been built on grade, for use either as more sleeping space or as a playroom.

Another simple way to create a maximum of living space with minimum cutting of the hillside is to cantilever the upper stories over the foundation as in the drawing.

By this design device a great deal of space can be added to a house—and dramatic design effects created. With perfectly conventional design and materials, overhangs or cantilevers as deep as eight feet can be created on one or both sides of a house. Houses that explore several cantilever effects are included in this chapter.

Because of the special nature of houses for steep sites, there are not many defined "rules" for the design of such houses—almost by definition they need to be special. But you'll find a few characteristics in the houses that follow:

1. They tend to emphasize their verticality by the use of vertical siding, by the use of tall windows, or by the use of strong vertical lines in the trim or exposed structure.

2. The slope of the hill tends to be echoed in the slope of the roof and, in some cases, by applying the siding in the end walls at the angle of the roof. These design devices tend to emphasize and support the strongest element of all—the hill itself.

3. You'll find decks galore—again because it is often simpler and cheaper (and usually more spectacular) to extend floor beams outside and create a deck than it is to arrange sliding glass doors opening to the natural grade.

4. Perhaps the most spectacular possible detail—and you'll see several versions in these houses—is the entry bridge reaching out from the hillside near the parking area and extending across space to a door that might, in a house like this, be on the third floor.

5. There are no hard-and-fast rules about what rooms go on what levels in a steep-site house. While convention cries for living rooms and dining rooms and kitchens to be on the first level, with the bedrooms above, who says it has to be that way? In a house like that in the sketch, it would be possible to walk all the way down the hill (in rain or snow) to a front door on grade, and then climb back up to living rooms. But . . .

The entry across the bridge is exciting. The best view is likely to be from the upper level. So why not enter on top, and then go downstairs to sleep?

So, fundamentally . . . no rules. If you've got the nerve to live on a site like this, find an architect who will make the most of the site with a house like one of these. And then have fun . . .

Norman McGrath photos

A STRIKING HOUSE THAT STEPS DOWN ITS HILLSIDE

A cool secluded pond is the focus for this house in the Green Mountains of Vermont. Access by car is possible only at a level 35 feet above the water, and so the entrance is at the top and the house is a series of terraced rooms facing the view and arranged around a central stairway that steps down inexorably from the entrance to the pond below, and just before (for the less adventurous) to an open deck and swimming pool.

Exigency as well as predilection controlled some of the decisions, too, for the house is made of standard 2 by 4 framing, with standard windows, doors, skylights, and commonly available sizes of plywood and sheetrock, installed with a minimum of cutting.

The architect points out that he was trying to put standard parts together in other than standard ways. This, admittedly, is not a unique intention today, as anything that veers even a single degree from the standard can skew the construction budget out of all recognition. Here, though, the attempt has worked: the house is not standard, and certainly doesn't look standard.

The long stairway, covered over by a 57-foot skylight, is a critical element among the special qualities of the house. From the outside, it helps bring the separate rooms together to make a single shape, and from the inside it performs a similar function. Flooded with sunlight, it allows movement up and down and across it, and even provides a place—an interior garden in the center of the house—for temporary repose; or for catching a passing glimpse of the sky or the water below.

Architect: Peter L. Gluck. *Owners:* Mr. and Mrs. B. Bookstaver. *Location:* Westminster, Vermont.

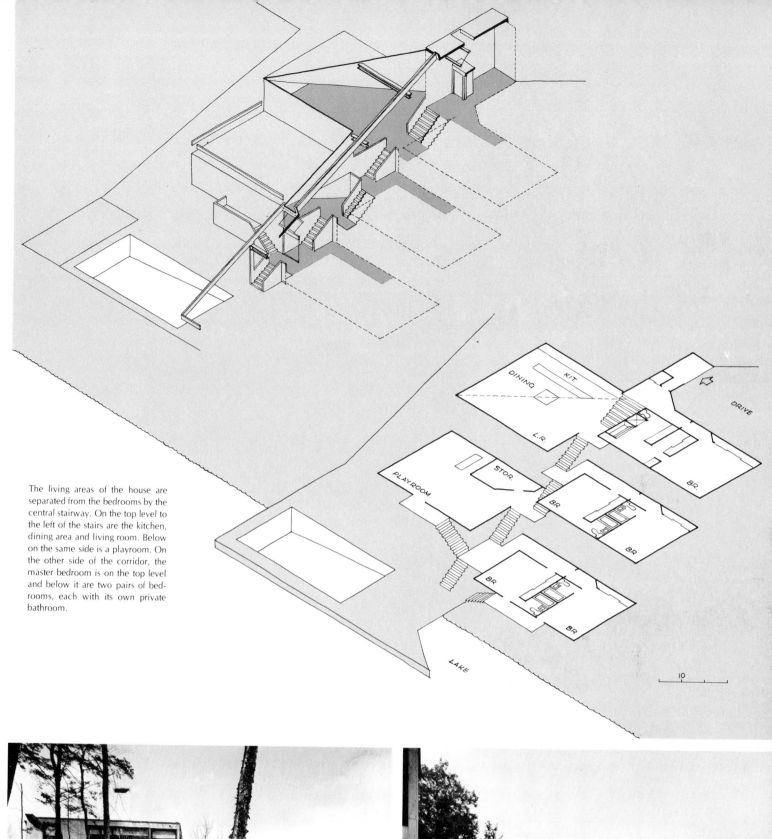

The living areas of the house are separated from the bedrooms by the central stairway. On the top level to the left of the stairs are the kitchen, dining area and living room. Below on the same side is a playroom. On the other side of the corridor, the master bedroom is on the top level and below it are two pairs of bedrooms, each with its own private bathroom.

DINING KIT L.R. DRIVE BR

PLAYROOM STOR. BR BR BR

BR BR

LAKE

10

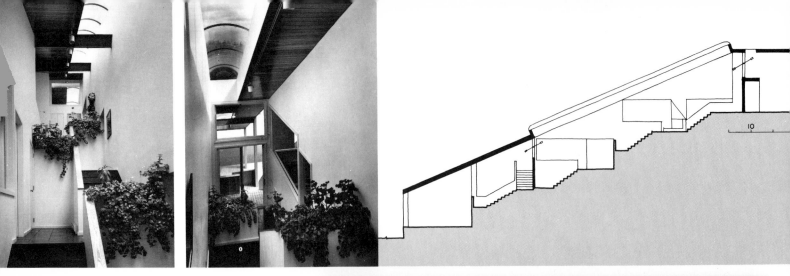

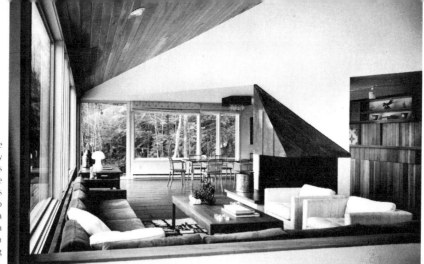

Near the entrance at the top of the house, the stairway opens directly into the living room (left), which is also seen on the right and above. The long skylight above the stairs allows solar heat generated in this space to rise to the top and exit through a large pivot window, creating a chimney effect. Outside air is drawn into the house from below, resulting in a natural air-conditioning system.

Joshua Freiwald photos

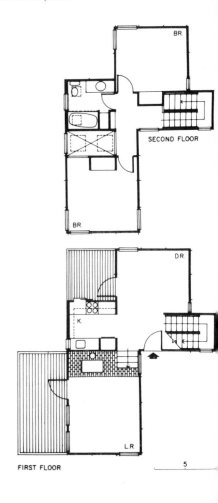

FIRST FLOOR

SECOND FLOOR

A MINIMUM-COST HOUSE
TUCKED INTO A HILLSIDE

This rugged and very original little house grew out of an attempt to provide a specially-designed low-cost vacation home in a beautiful but remote area where building costs are high. It uses prefabricated stressed-skin panels for walls and floors, for an estimated 15 per cent saving over conventional wood frame. In addition to the Record Houses award winner, which was built for sale (right), two even lower-priced versions have been built, shown at left.

The patented structural panels consist of a plywood skin and a rigid, fire-resistant foam plastic core. The core insulates, and the plywood—redwood on the exterior and cedar or fir inside—also forms the finish.

The panels are four feet wide, and the real key to success came in using this module as the basis for efficient plans. The larger house has a 932-square-foot living area. It cost $15,000 in 1968, including a fully-equipped kitchen and bathroom, wall-to-wall indoor-outdoor carpets and electric floor and baseboard unit heating. The second, smaller house to the top left cost $12,000; the third, costing $10,000, was achieved with sleeping alcoves and the use of outdoor decks. Details for all three were designed to scuttle complicated on-site construction steps, and use simple joints and simple finishes from stock materials to help keep costs in line. The larger house took just three days to build, using a four-man crew.

Architect and *owner*: Sim Van der Ryn of Hirshen & Van der Ryn. *Location*: Point Reyes, California. *Contractor*: W. D. McAlvain.

FIRST FLOOR   SECOND FLOOR

A number of playful "extras" are built into the two-story, split-level design: The living room with its Franklin stove has a skylit, two-story "well." An overlook from the kitchen can be seen in the photos (below). Wherever possible, outdoor decks are enlisted to increase living space without adding to foundation costs.

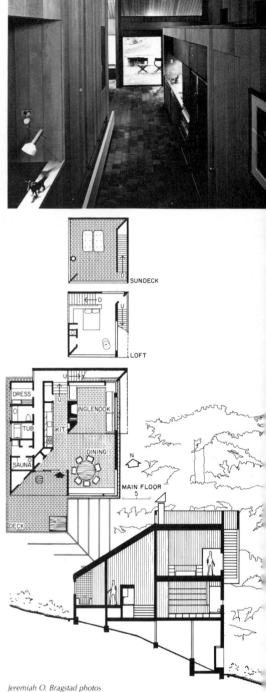

SUNDECK

LOFT

DRESS

INGLENOOK

TUB

KIT

SAUNA

DINING

N

MAIN FLOOR

DECK

Jeremiah O. Bragstad photos

FROM ABOVE, A COTTAGE: FROM BELOW, A TOWER

An indigenous material and a modest form have been combined to produce an intriguing yet uncomplicated vacation house. Architects McCue Boone Tomsick make the most of a downhill approach (above) by sheathing the roof as well as the walls with tongue-and-groove redwood boards. The unifying effect of the common material makes the house seem smaller and more simple than it proves to be upon entry (acrosspage). Yet such modesty is entirely appropriate when the site is an isolated and heavily forested hillside in the Santa Cruz Moutains of California, looking out over a valley preserve toward the Pacific Ocean. The angled wall, which follows the hip of the roof at the entry, provides protected entrance where those who

have walked down the hill from the parking area may remove muddy boots and winter coats before entering. That part of the house is oriented away from the winds but catches mid-day sun. End-grain redwood paving blocks form a parquet terrace that continues indoors as an important finish.

A very generous stairway within the single, large interior space makes vertical circulation an important generator of the functional relationships. Directly ahead, as one enters, a short flight of steps just past the kitchen leads to the level with four small rooms containing toilet facilities (including a sauna). To the right and up the stairs is the bedroom. Again to the right, and now outdoors, this squared spiral leads up to the sun-

deck in the treetops. Redwood boards also sheathe the interior completely; the ceiling boards are spaced slightly apart to assist in ventilation of the roof structure. Although the large space is beautifully detailed, it is clear that it was designed for unpretentious and relaxed vacation use. Within the large space, the eating area is adjacent to the strip kitchen. Under the ceiling formed by the bedroom floor, is an inglenook sitting area around a fireplace whose seating doubles as extra sleeping accommodation.

Architects: McCue Boone Tomsick. *Location:* San Mateo County, California. *Engineers:* Hirsh and Gray (structural); Marion, Cerbatos and Tomasi (mechanical/electrical). *General contractor:* Henry Knutzen Sons, Inc.

A high degree of spatial integration is achieved within the house by the use of a single material—redwood—on walls, ceilings and floors. The square spiral stairway and the loft bedroom which opens onto the large space below also contribute to the unified feeling. Butted glazing in both downhill corner windows of the main floor room provide splendid diagonal views into the thick foliage while the slit windows illuminate the page for anyone reading on the built-in couch.

Three bays thrusting out from the line of the foundation wall create tree-house spaces throughout this hillside house. Photo near right is the living room, with a built-in couch that provides three-way views. Above it is an open deck let into the roof and reached from the upper-level entryway. Photo beyond shows the master bedroom and study. The use of mitred glass in the corners of bays of course reinforces the sense of lightness and extension out over the site which make these rooms so exciting.

A HOUSE CANTILEVERED ABOVE A MINIMUM FOUNDATION

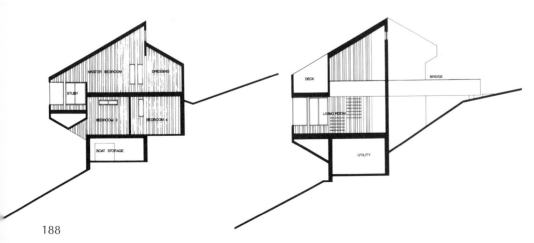

In every part of its conception, design, and construction, this house is inventively, ingeniously, and most pleasantly related to its steep and heavily wooded site in Sherman, Connecticut.

To begin with, excavation on the hillside was minimized by the form of the house (see sections, left). At the living room end of the house (near section, bottom in plans above) the footings are only 12 feet apart; at the other end of the house (far section) somewhat more—but never extensive—cutting and a third foundation wall

Co-designers: Norman Jaffe, A.I.A., and Nicos Zographos.
Owner: Carl Fisher. Location: Sherman, Connecticut. Contractor: Clifford Hirsch.

was used to fit lower level rooms into the slope.

On the downhill side of the house, the living area is extended beyond the foundation wall by simply extending the floor joists and bracing them with 2 x 6's that return to the foundation, creating the two big (8-foot deep) and one small "bay" shown in the photos at the top of the page. The two big bays differ in depth, as the photo above shows most clearly, reflecting the side slope of the hill.

The house is entered by a bridge on the uphill side (see plan and section). One turns right to the kitchen and dining area, with its table set in the small bay.

Beyond is the master suite, with a compartmented bath and—down five steps following the slope of the roof and the hill—a tree-house study, set in the smaller of the two bays (see photo above).

From the entryway to the left is a balcony overlooking the two-story living room and leading to an open deck let into the roof of the larger bay (near section). Stairs lead down from the balcony to the living

room (photo left above) which extends into the bay for three-way views of the site. Three more bedrooms, a compartmented bath and a sauna are also located on the lower level.

All of the finishes, inside and out, are natural wood, most appropriate to the site. Interior walls and ceilings are rough-sawn cypress, floors are oak, and the exterior is cedar shingle.

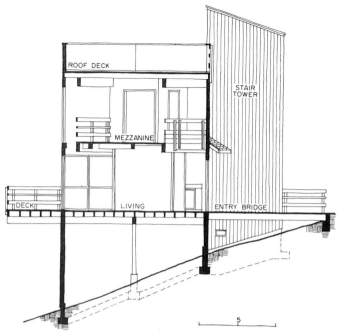

THIS HOUSE
GETS SPACE
BY GOING UP,
NOT OUT

This low-budget vacation house at the Sea Ranch, a complex of vacation homes north of San Francisco overlooking the Mendocino coast line, was built as a prototype to show prospective buyers the sort of house that might be built on a steep, heavily wooded hillside lot with a distant view of the water. The house is a festive and simple one-room hexagonal tower with an attached stair tower. The stairs lead to a sleeping-shelf mezzanine with bath, and then on to a roof deck with a magnificent view. The main level, containing living room, kitchen and porch, is entered via a bridge, with the entrance sheltered by a canopy roof. The exterior is horizontally- and vertically-applied redwood treated with bleaching oil; with a built-up roof and duck board decking. Interior walls are fir and plywood, with ceilings of exposed fir beams and decking of plywood. The house is designed for any number of steep, wooded lots (two examples have been completed), and is expandable by adding hexagons.

Architect: Marquis and Stoller—Pete Kampf, associates. *Location:* The Sea Ranch, Sonoma County, California. *Engineer:* Eric Elsesser. *Contractor:* Matthew Sylvia.

MEZZANINE FLOOR

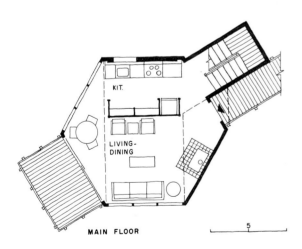

KIT.

LIVING-
DINING

MAIN FLOOR

5

A sleeping deck over-
looks the two-story living
room in this vertically-
organized octagonal
house for a steep,
wooded site.

8: Houses for flat sites

In the earlier chapters of this book, we've discussed houses for what might be called "the exciting sites"—sites with great views, sites on or near beach or lake, broad and beautiful meadows, sites deep in the woods, sites that slope with varying degrees of drama down the nation's hillsides and mountainsides.

And so we come to perhaps the commonest and most ubiquitous kind of site in America: the flat site. Must you despair—having enjoyed the exciting cliff-hangers of the previous pages—if you live in any of those many states in America which offer little but flat sites? Or if the lot you own, even if it is in Vermont or Colorado, happens to be flat?

The answer, of course, is of course not.

It is probably fair to say that it is more difficult to create an exciting and dramatic house on a flat piece of land than it is on a beach or a mountainside. The excitement, the drama, does not come with the deed—it has to be created. But—as the houses in these final pages show—good architects are very good indeed at creating that drama for those families who want it and will give their architect the license to create it for them.

How does a good architect create the excitement? As in meadow sites, you can treat the house as a piece of sculpture placed on the site. Sometimes (as in the house on the next pages) it can be given a strong and fanciful shape, with strong sloping skylights and roofs set in varying planes. The second house in this section is again a strong composition, but that strength is created in a very different way. Here the roof is flat, and the excitement is created by strong angles in the plan—using a parallelogram instead of a rectangle as the essential shape—and by setting off great sheets of glass against equally bold solid panels of wood. In the third house (pages 200–203), we see yet another way to create excitement and drama—in this case in a relatively simple and lower-cost house. Its form is an almost perfect cube, 30 feet on a side, with a flat roof. But here the architect carved away sections of the cube to create decks and a greenhouse and a very strong two-story living room, and placed the glass so that at night (as the color photo on page 200 shows) the house fairly glistens.

In general, the houses in this flat-site section are quite tall, to create a strong presence. In contrast to woodland houses, which, as mentioned before, tend to be designed so they blend into the site, these houses tend to be designed to stand out. A broader palette of materials has been used—in this group you will find horizontal and/or vertical siding, brick, stone, white-painted panels. Strong design elements like heavy decks (or, in reverse, heavy cut-outs in the basic building mass) are common.

As if to counteract the flatness of these sites, almost all of these houses have something exciting going on inside. Several have two-story living spaces, some topped with dramatic skylights. In others, the floor levels are not set conventionally—rather, beginning on the main floor, there is a progression upwards to rooms on multiple levels. Light is funneled deep into the living spaces by unexpected light scoops or skylights. Even, as the four-color photos show, bright colors have a special role in this kind of house—again, on the philosophy that if excitement didn't come with the site, a greater effort must be made to design it into the house.

Maris-Semel photos

SLOPED FORMS RISING FROM A FLAT FIELD

This house in Bridgehampton, Long Island, for a family of four, rises in a striking series of sloped forms with complex faceting and rather intricate internal spaces. Earth berms, at front and rear, ease the transition between the level site and the three-story structure. On the lower level, children's bedrooms are grouped around a recreational space. The middle level contains the main living spaces while the master bedroom and bath occupy the top level. The upper two levels, connected by a stair and a vertical shaft of space, provide welcome views of the ocean to the north. It is a house with outdoor spaces on two levels and views from the upper levels in every direction. The principal exterior finish materials are stucco and gray-stained cedar boards. Inside, the finishes include plaster board, light wood trim, and clay tile used selectively in the kitchen.

Like the others in this group, this house draws its strength from the forcefulness of its forms and the skill with which the major spaces have been shaped. The succession of low-ceilinged spaces leading to the double-height living room (overleaf) is a vigorous spatial composition, sculptured at the top by inclined forms. The sense of openness and the easy flow of spaces extends almost effortlessly through sliding glass doors to the view beyond. It is a personal house, to be sure, and a house that is idiosyncratic, but nowhere does the design look unresolved or the planning timid—a tribute both to the architect and the owner.

Architect: Alfred De Vido. *Location:* Bridgehampton, New York. *Interior designer:* Juan Mir. *Contractor:* Peter Wazlo, Inc.

SECOND FLOOR

STUDY   L.R.

KIT.

D.R.

MAIN FLOOR

STOR.

RECREATION

5

BR.   BR.   GROUND FLOOR

Like the exteriors, the interiors are conceived and executed without undue restraint. Colors get their full value and many design elements are treated as opportunities for architectural sculpture. Several of the photographs (left and above) indicate the effects of natural light introduced deep into interior spaces from unexpected sources overhead.

SECOND FLOOR

FIRST FLOOR

STRIKING SHAPES AND COLORS ON A FLAT SITE

The strict rectilinear geometry of this handsome house in Armonk, New York, by architects Mayers & Schiff, is modified by a parallelogram-shaped enclosure applied to its eastern side. The two-story parallelogram which extends and unifies the rectangular spaces, contains the entry with a small study above. It also houses, on the lower level, a long built-in cabinet for hi-fi, storage, seating and grilles. Over this cabinet, which runs nearly the full length of the house, hangs a bank of theatrical border lights, painted bright yellow, that provides the interiors with an unexpected but forceful sculptural element. Off the entry, and

partially concealed by the mass of the fireplace, a circular stair leads to bedrooms on the gallery level above—bedrooms that open through slit windows to grand views of trees and the surrounding site.

The exterior is wood frame, clad in redwood siding bleached to an off-white. The floor is oak strip and interior partitions are finished in vinyl wall covering.

The house is remarkable for its spatial liveliness, the sparkling transparency with which it opens to its wooded site, and the formal elegance it achieves with a relatively few, carefully measured elements and design flourishes. It is a house that offers its

occupants a rich variety of visual stimulants but affords, at the same time, easy avenues of visual release. It is a house that excites tactile senses too, but the textures do not come at the expense of livability. The detailing and sensible selection of finish materials should insure continuing good looks with only routine, simple maintenance and minimal upkeep.

Architects: Mayers & Schiff. *Location:* Armonk, New York. *Engineers:* Wolchuk & Mayrbaurl (structural); Robert Freudenberg (electrical). *Contractor:* William A. Kelly & Company.

Maris-Sempel photos

Photos, left and right, show the two-story volume created at the juncture between the parallelogram and the rectilinear volumes. At left: partial view of living room and bedroom gallery above. At right: the small study framed against a background of trees. This study can be closed from the bedroom areas by a sliding partition (see plan, opposite page).

Otto Baitz photos

CUT-OUTS FROM A CUBE CREATE A STRIKING FORM

Home-made houses have an important place in American tradition. But few ever claim to be architecture. However this 30-foot cube, set gently into nature not far from Woodstock, seems to combine the wholesome ingenuousness of the *Whole Earth Catalogue* with the formal purity of Ledoux's visionary projects of the 18th century.

The powerful geometry of the cube, unexpected in a rural place, overrides simple construction techniques—plywood on a steel and wood frame—and the resultant effect is one of freedom within order, old living happily with new. For instance, the crusty small-paned window panels, right, were taken from a nearby greenhouse about to be destroyed and incorporated into the house as it was being built.

All of this could seem quite contrived if it did not so accurately represent the lifestyle of the owners. The chaplain of Bard College and his wife, a serious pianist, are two mature and highly sophisticated people. They needed a house that would not impose a regime on them but rather would easily accept their existing pattern of living. But neither would their budget allow for one of those spacious houses that have a specially-designed room for everything.

The product of that program was built largely by the family with their son, Paul Shafer, in charge. It stands just ten feet from a rushing stream. In the spring flood waters come under the house but other times the brook seems to go out of its way to skirt the building. The 45-degree glazed corners enable a person standing next to the center-post of the house on the mezzanine to look out of the dining room window and see the stream approaching, then turn clockwise to watch it pass the tall living room window. Finally, turning another 90 degrees, he sees it disappear over the falls just below the house.

Architects: *James B. Baker of Baker and Blake. Associate architect: Alex Wade. Owners: Rev. and Mrs. Frederick Q. Shafer. Location: Annandale-on-Hudson, New York. Structural engineer: Robert Silman. Mechanical engineers: Flack and Kurtz. Contractor (foundations and steel erection): Dittmar and Regg.*

Each floor of the three-story house has a distinctly different quality. The spacious living room, lowest floor, has two low areas, the conservatory and fireplace corners, joined by a two-story space. The kitchen and dining room seem small in comparison but share both the tall space and the light which pours in from every side. The top floor, divided into many small rooms, provides a private place for each person.

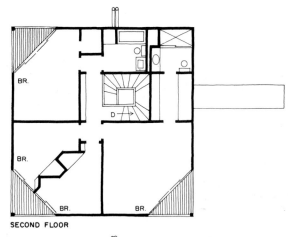

SECOND FLOOR

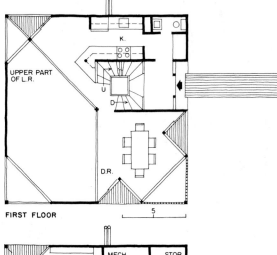

FIRST FLOOR

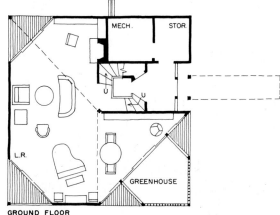

GROUND FLOOR

The two primary functions of the house, openness to nature and service of highly-developed lifestyles, are apparent on the interior. As one approaches the entrance, above left, on the bridge, the transparency of the house is conveyed by the multi-faceted glazing of the conservatory and above it, the dining room. From the entry, one goes down half-a-flight on the suspended plywood stair, top, to the living room or up to the dining room. The slender post in the middle of the house, above, is four steel angles. The furniture and objets d'art of the house, opposite, highly personal but displayed with assuredness, convey the diversity of the life lived here.

COMPLEX FORMS
FOR DRAMA
ON A FLAT SITE

"Overlapping sheds with skylight spaces between forms" is Clovis Heimsath's description of his design concept for this house, which was built in Houston for a sculptor and his family. A strictly limited budget and the requirement for two studios in addition to comfortable family living areas made this a challenging program for the architect. Mr. Heimsath solved the problems by adopting a shed roof motif which allowed sufficient height and volume for the creation of exciting two-story spaces and constantly changing patterns of light and shade inside and out.

Visual continuity of space between floors was very important since budget restrictions limited floor area, but a "row of little rooms" would have been functionally and esthetically unacceptable to the clients and the architect. The height was emphasized by strategically placed skylights which serve to extend the experience of space.

The first two-story space is the dramatic entry which is spanned by the hall on the second floor; the upstairs studio is a balcony above the sculpture studio on the lower level. The third two-story dimension is provided by the master bedroom which overlooks part of the living room.

The plan was developed around a central core, which consists of washer-dryer facilities and a powder room downstairs, two bathrooms above and necessary ductwork. The architect insists that this is where the scheme started. He says: "The design truly developed from plan to form. The clients had two children and might later add to the family, so the plan had to have three bedrooms, two studios, two and a half baths, living room and

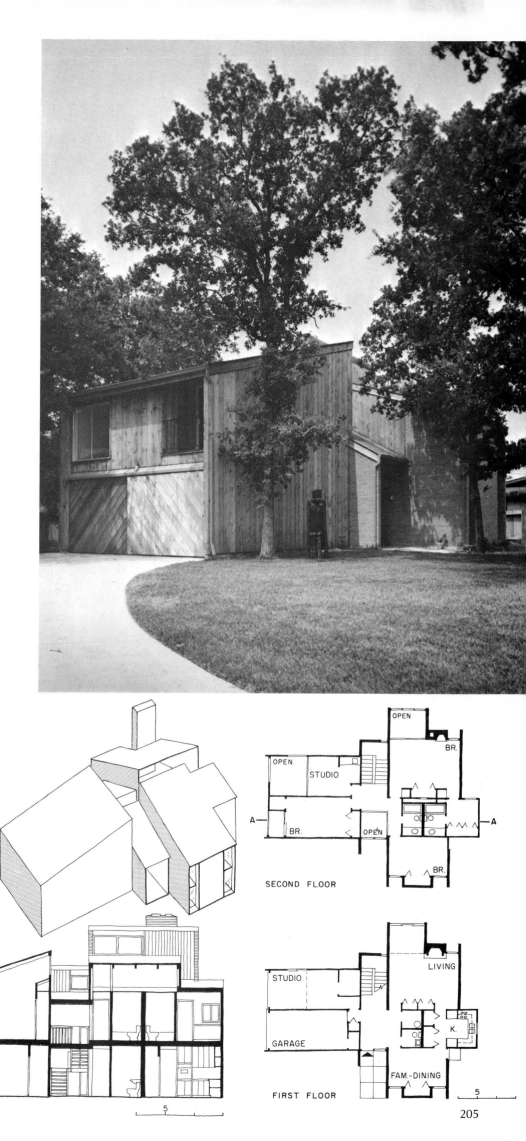

SECOND FLOOR

SECTION A-A

FIRST FLOOR

family-dining room. I started with the core and from there evolved a plan which placed the kitchen and family-dining room on one side, and the living room on the other. Upstairs the master bedroom and one other bedroom are separated by the bathrooms. The hallway had to be minimum, so the entry-stair hall relationship fell in place. It was at this point that the shed roof motif seemed appropriate to give me volumetric space, and to allow skylight spaces between the forms."

Mr. Heimsath says that he had some difficulty in deciding how to relate the studio wing with the rest of the house. The massing of the other forms built up into a "counter thrusting" relationship, but the studio wing had nothing to counter thrust against. It was therefore turned around "to play off against the rest of the house. Then it worked." The resulting scheme has a rather compact, sculptural effect, but the many skylights give it life and interest and save it from being too inward-looking.

Mr. Heimsath is convinced that no two rooms in one house should have the same spatial impact. By placing storage on the exterior wall of the family room—in contrast to the living room where it is on the interior wall, with the fireplace on the outside—he was able to vary the interior spaces and at the same time provide sufficient exterior massing to offset the dominance of the shed forms.

Architect: Clovis Heimsath; *Owner:* Mr. and Mrs. Robert K. Fowler, Jr.; *Location:* Houston; *Contractor:* W. A. Simmons

A certain amount of flexibility was provided by making the ground floor studio convertible to a garage if necessary, and the upstairs studio to a fourth bedroom if required. The house is set diagonally on its site, allowing a view up a bayou on one side. From the balcony of the children's bedroom above the garage, there is a pleasant outlook up the tree-lined street. Exterior materials of brick, rough-cedar and glass are well detailed and carefully related to each other.

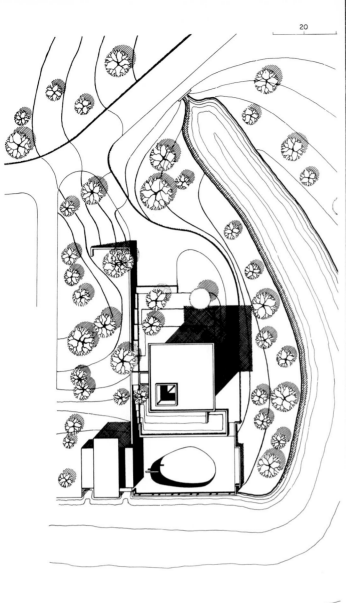

A CUBE-SHAPED HOUSE WITH EXPANDED SPACES

For a woodland site on a small Florida peninsula, William Morgan designed a cube-shaped house whose height permits a sweeping river view through the surrounding trees, and whose small ground area preserves the existing live-oak woods intact. On closer inspection, and in the following pages, this familiar shape, solidly anchored to its site, opens up into new spaces, expanded and unexpected.

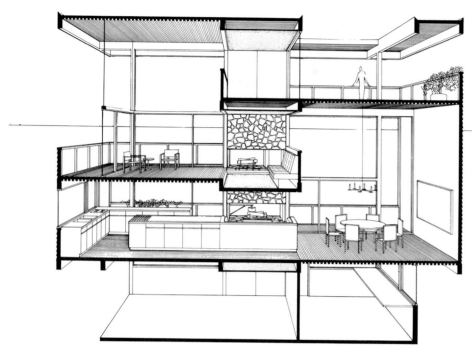

Varied floor levels, spirally arranged in a vigorous interplay of interior spaces, are actually geared to strategic views and controlled by the logic of a four-story grid plan. Rooms in section appear in white on plans.

THIRD FLOOR

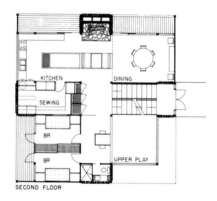

SECOND FLOOR

FOURTH FLOOR

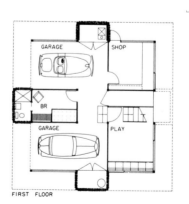

FIRST FLOOR

William Morgan has treated this house in Jacksonville, Florida in a delightfully unorthodox manner. Two-story spaces are spiralled within the cube. The result is an exciting interplay to be discovered behind a placid, compact exterior.

The key to this house's intriguing contrast of open, varied space and defining shape—and to its structure—are the four stone-faced columns. Already familiar elements in Morgan's work, they are used with great sophistication. As structural supports they not only permit variations in ceiling height (from 6 feet, 8 inches to 14 feet 7 inches) and much open living area (4,060 square feet in four levels); but, doubling as service towers, they concentrate fireplace, stairs, air conditioning and plumbing into neat vertical packages, leaving the living areas uncluttered. Utility chases which connect the structural columns are hidden under

The staggered levels within are expressed as patterns on the exterior. These varied facades are secured by the firm verticals of the structural towers and by the strong line of the roof. Recessed glass panels and broad overhangs that protect against direct sunlight form bold patterns of light and dense shadow. South and east from the living room, and south from the dining room, are the main glass areas, which open two full stories to the river basin.

A low-ceilinged inglenook (below) sets off the living room's two-story height, while to the rear a balcony reveals the second great space—of the dining room—beyond.

Alexandre Georges photos

The dressing room of the Hatcher house (right) is located on the closed-off north side, as are other private and quiet areas (guest and master bedrooms, study). Careful lighting design emphasizes the boldly detailed, exposed beams and floor-ceiling deck. Dining room and kitchen (below left), actually form a single expanse; their areas are defined by a change in ceiling height.

dropped ceilings. The 6- by 12-inch beams between the four columns are supported by 6- by 6-inch posts.

Exposed structural members and natural-finished materials add to the interior clarity and sense of continuity between outside and inside. Floor decking, of 2-inch by 4-inch edge grain pine alternating with 2-inch by 3-inch spacers, is exposed below, forming finished ceilings. Wood siding of clear cypress, dressed and matched in a narrow horizontal board pattern, blends warmly with the facing stone of light brown coquina rock, locally quarried. Matching siding is used for the low boathouse and relates this outlying building to the main block of the house.

The house is sparingly furnished to emphasize the sweeping views, the varied spaces, the natural-finished cypress and pine-wood textures, and the clean de Stijl-like intersections of planes.

Architect: William Morgan. *Owners:* Mr. and Mrs. William K. Hatcher. *Location:* Jacksonville, Florida. *Engineers:* Haley Keister. *Contractor:* Ross Construction Co.

A final word:

decisions, decisions

When you have finished studying this book, you may be disappointed that you have not found a house that is just right for you and your family.

You should not be surprised. For all of the houses in this book were designed by architects for families that are not the same as yours—families that do not have the same interests, the same prejudices, the same priorities. These houses were for *them,* not you.

If you are seriously thinking about a house for you, on your kind of site, for your kind of living, find an architect to share your dreams with. It's hard to tell you how to choose one. You should admire the earlier work he has done. You should like him (or her) as a person—because yours will be a very personal relationship. Before he even puts a pencil to paper, he has to learn about you. And he is going to have to force you to make a lot of decisions about your priorities—you can't have everything you want, and you have to decide what you want most. After all of that probing and searching and questioning . . . · then he does his thing as a designer.

For both you and your architect, it is a difficult process, sometimes frustrating, sometimes confusing. But when you and he are finished, you have one of the best things any person or family can have: *your* house. A house that is just right for you. And, as the saying goes, you will live happily ever after.

Index

213